Media Handbook for Churches

Books by Charles Somervill
published by The Westminster Press

With Kerry L. Townson
Media Handbook for Churches

With H. Wayland Cummings
Leadership Strategies for Ministers

Media Handbook for Churches

Charles Somervill
and
Kerry L. Townson

The Westminster Press
Philadelphia

First edition

Published by The Westminster Press®
Philadelphia, Pennsylvania

PRINTED IN THE UNITED STATES OF AMERICA

9 8 7 6 5 4 3 2 1

Library of Congress Cataloging-in-Publication Data

Somervill, Charles.
  Media handbook for churches / Charles Somervill and Kerry L. Townson. — 1st ed.
      p.   cm.
  Bibliography: p.
  ISBN 0-664-25029-7 (pbk.)

  1. Mass media in religion. I. Townson, Kerry L. (Kerry Lyle), 1957–   . II. Title.
BV652.95.S64 1988
254.3—dc19   88-6086
                                                                         CIP

We dedicate this book
to the women we dearly love
at work and at home—

To Paula, Mollie, Wendy,
and especially our boss,
Flora Fenner French

Contents

We gratefully acknowledge the help and expertise of Kayleen Barbe, Harold Bretz, Marj Carpenter, Wayland Cummings, Mollie Fennell, Wes Jackson, Thom McCain, Arden Moser, Betty Redman, and Robert Shelton.

Introduction

The new technology, in some ways, has exceeded the expectations of the book *1984*. There have been many changes. Children are learning on computers, cable TV has stretched its network across the United States, satellites have linked nations closer together, and electronic gadgets sold in local stores continue to amaze us. A simple wristwatch not only gives the time and date but can keep track of your appointments, record telephone numbers, do your arithmetic, and wake you up in the mornings—and that by no means exhausts the list. With so much information suddenly at our fingertips, the term "information revolution" has given way to "information explosion."

However, contrary to the depiction in *1984*, the new technology with its information explosion has probably done more to enhance freedom, at least in the United States, than to limit it. The ease with which we obtain information is directly related to a well-informed society, the cornerstone of democracy.

The mission of the church also strongly depends on its ability to send and receive messages. The media with their hi-tech advancements offer the church a set of tools to proclaim the good news as never before. First attempts may be clumsy and poorly produced, but they are nothing to be embarrassed about. They are all part of learning and well worth the effort.

In many larger communities, for example, access cable television offers free channels to the churches. Usually these channels are reserved for local programming. Access is a carryover from the days of public service announcements and "programming in the public interest." Furthermore, access offers the unique opportunity of "narrowcasting" to small groups as well as "broadcasting" to larger audiences. (Narrowcasting is a generic term, not limited to closed-circuit TV, which refers to any program intended for a small audience—even though the channel may be open to a larger one.) Because cable TV presents an abundance of channels, television need no longer be regarded as a scarce resource reserved for mass audiences.

Many churches who have discovered narrowcasting via access TV already are producing programs intended for such small audiences as those found in church officers' training groups and vacation church schools, curriculum review for church school teachers, reports on denominational meetings, and similar events. This type of programming, of course, is exactly the same as the in-house productions used within the church. Such programs have a double use, providing copies for both the video library of the church and of the access channel. The authors, both of whom have extensive experience in access TV, have seen a number of churches use their internal resources in just this way. When one understands a few simple principles—provided in this book—about lighting, sound, and editing, producing TV programs becomes easy and interesting.

Television is a powerful medium because it links sight to sound. The more senses a medium engages, the stronger its appeal and the stronger our participation. But the church would be mistaken to limit its outreach to TV. A multimedia approach is far superior to the use of a single medium. Print engages sight and allows for instant replay of information. The radio only requires listening and permits its audience the freedom to do other things, such as driving. The more ways we are exposed to the same information, the greater our awareness and memory of it. A church that truly desires to be understood will seek to make use of all available media.

An active media or communication committee in the church can be one of the most valuable groups of people within the congregation. Of course, it probably is wisest to inaugurate such a committee as an integral part of the church's organization with the blessings and support of the official governing body. The media committee has an important adjunct function to the work of the other committees in the church. It is not so much a program of the church as it is a proclaimer of other programs. Ideally, the members of this committee should have a variety of talents, ranging from creative writing and dramatics to technical skills in electronics.

The narrative of this book looks over the shoulders of a fictitious media committee at First Church whose members have very few resources within the congregation. They have some enthusiasm for using media but not much idea of what they are getting into or what steps to take. Their cheerfully persistent chairperson, Harriet Wingate, leads them into a use of media that opens large windows at First Church.

It takes time and planning to develop a systematic use of media that significantly improves communication within both church and community. Once a church learns how to do this, however, it will probably want to make these activities a permanent part of the budget. Very few investments yield such generous dividends. Developing this process of using media is the goal of *Media Handbook for Churches.*

1

Preparing for Media Usage

When a media committee has just been selected from a congregation, what happens next? Often the members of such a committee have different ideas about how to use media. Some members may want to concentrate on church advertising. Others may contend that the focus of their efforts should be on improving communications within the congregation. Still others may insist that the primary purpose of media is to furnish an extension of the church's ministry into the community. Priorities have to be set so that the committee will not bog down in frustration.

A logical way to proceed is to examine the purpose, cost, and effectiveness of the different types of media. Consider a fictitious media committee at First Church, meeting for the second time. The first meeting was spent getting to know one another and electing a chairperson, Harriet Wingate. Each person was assigned an area to investigate and report on for this second meeting.

Developing a media committee

"We are here to discuss the most effective use of media for the small amount of money we have in the budget," Harriet began. "Who wants to begin?"

Mark Johnson spoke up first. "I would like to suggest that we develop a campaign for church advertising. We need to let people in the community know who we are and what we stand for. An organization that doesn't advertise can't survive."

Harold Jordan objected. "Our church has gotten along without advertising for years," he said. "We're not going to get any more people in the pews by running an ad in the paper. Most folks won't even see it, and the ones who do aren't going to come to church on the strength of an ad."

"Then why do companies advertise?" asked Mark.

"Because they've got a product to sell. What's our product?"

"Fellowship, friendship with God, worship—"

"None of which makes us different from any other church," Harold said. "Besides that, our product is not something tangible. There's no sizzle to sell."

"Wouldn't people respond to an ad that tells about a congregation of loving, friendly people?" Jane Hardgrove asked.

"Well-I." Harold deliberated. "Let's suppose I put an ad in the paper, beautifully laid out, with a picture of the church, that eloquently describes the group of wonderful people we have here. You've never heard of our church before, but you know how advertising exaggerates. Jane, are you telling me you would come to my church because of that ad?"

"Well, I might."

"You'd be one in a million," Harold said. "And the same thing would be true with radio and television—church ads don't work. I've never responded to one, and I don't think any of you have either."

"OK, I'll admit I've never responded to a church ad," Mark said, "but if what you say is true, why are we meeting here?"

"Maybe we'd better move on to another area and come back to church advertising," Harriet suggested.

Martha Randels took up the challenge. "I think we need to talk about media as an extension of our ministry into the community. I'm not talking about advertising. What we should look at is a radio or TV ministry."

"Have you considered the costs?" Harold asked, ever practical.

"No, but think of the possibilities."

Mark reluctantly agreed with Harold. "The costs would be astronomical. We could never afford it."

"Then what can our committee do?" Martha wanted to know.

"There is such a thing as a free TV channel on public access," Harriet told her.

"And who's going to do the production?" Harold retorted. "The channel may be free, but what about the equipment to produce the program?"

"Obviously, we need more information," Harriet said. "But I'm not giving up. We're going to find a way to make this committee work."

"We still haven't discussed the use of media *within* the church," Bill Henson announced. "Our church newsletter could use some improvement, and there may be a way of using videotapes for the church school and other meetings."

"Let me tell you what you are getting into there—" began Harold.

"No, Harold." Harriet laughed. "I am *not* going to let you shoot down another idea. I'm going to suggest that we end the meeting now and take a different approach next time we meet."

Harold folded his arms and smiled. "It better be good."

"You wait and see." Harriet put her hand on Harold's shoulder. "I'm bringing a guest expert to our meeting next time who may be able to answer some of your objections. Other churches have media committees, and they must be doing something right. We're not going to give up."

Harriet was disappointed in the lack of information obtained by the committee members. Perhaps, she thought, they just didn't know where to get the facts. She went home and made a list of people she knew who had expertise in communications. Her list was short: a journalist, a TV studio production manager, and a communications professor. She made a note to herself to ask the other members of her media committee for the names of potential resource people. She suspected that many of the early committee meetings would benefit from outside advisers.

Using resource people

Harriet needed someone to motivate her members and provide a framework to get them working. She chose the communications professor, Dr. Sharon Norris, a well-known member of another church in the same denomination. After briefing Sharon, Harriet was ready for her next meeting.

"I'm not sure I can answer all your questions," Sharon told the media committee. "I know you are wondering what the media can do for your church within a limited budget. Let's begin with what we know about the media through research."

"What kind of research?" Harold asked.

"Studies on media effects and influence. Media research began in the fifties; there have been hundreds of studies, exploring everything from effects of the media to the broader picture of media impact on society."

Media effects

"Let me guess what you found out." Harold smiled. "Monkey see, monkey do. People watch television and are shaped by it."

"That's *not* what the research indicates," Sharon said. "I know that many people believe that media, especially TV, are like powerful syringes injecting the viewer. That's called the hypodermic theory, but it's not supported by the findings. What we have discovered is that media create two main effects: first, awareness, and second, reinforcement of existing values."

"Where does that leave us?" Mark asked.

"Well, what we are doing here in this small group probably is more effective for influencing people than television," Sharon said.

"What do you mean?" Jane was puzzled. "How can a small group have more influence than TV?"

"The way people are most influenced is by talking with other people they respect," Sharon replied. "Parental influence, peer attitudes, even the opinions of other church members are much more apt to change us than media."

"I agree." Harold leaned forward, interested. "So what good is our media committee?"

"Oh, the media have power, and, when used correctly, they can benefit the church in ways nothing else can," Sharon responded. *"Awareness* is the first step toward attitude change,

Awareness effect

and using the media is the most efficient way of creating awareness. I'm not going to attend your church just because I'm aware of it. However, if I'm not aware of it, you have no chance of reaching me at all."

"So awareness is necessary, but it has to be followed up with something else to get you through the door," Jane said.

"Yes, and probably you know the next step," Sharon replied. "I have to talk with someone else about it. For example, if I see something about your church in the paper, I might comment on it to Harriet. I might say, 'Harriet, I see your church is planning a special celebration this Sunday.' And Harriet, if she likes her church, would say, 'Yes. Why don't you come with me?'"

"Well, you might say something to Harriet or you might not." Harold laughed. "There's no guarantee you'll do anything because of a church notice."

"What using the media gives you is the possibility of my taking that next step," Sharon responded. "Sure, I might not talk to Harriet, but I'm certainly not going to say *anything* without becoming aware of your event through media exposure."

"I can see how that might work for an event," Harold said,

"but what good are *repeated* general advertisements—location, time of services, slogans?"

"That brings us to the second well-documented effect of the media: *reinforcement,*" Sharon continued. "The more often I see something, the greater my awareness and the more likely I am to talk about it."

Reinforcement effect

"Are awareness and reinforcement the only effects of media?" Mark asked. "Could the research have missed something? Look at it another way. We are constantly bombarded with messages, and the tube is on all the time in many homes. That has to have an impact."

"That's a good point," Sharon agreed. "In fact, media research today may be less interested in the obvious effects of media and more concerned with the larger picture of the influence of media on society. There is a growing body of evidence that suggests a sort of shaping effect on people. People select what they want to see in terms of their own values. But then, especially if they watch a lot of television, media *defines a social reality* for them."

Harold was intrigued. "What do you mean by social reality?"

"Well." Sharon thought for a moment. "It's a perceived reality that apparently television can create from programs we

A definer of social reality

select. For example, if you are a religious person who watches television, probably you will select at least some shows with a religious content. But suppose the religious shows on the air differ somewhat from what you believe?"

"If they were *too* different, I'd change the channel," Harold said.

"But if you perceive those differences as tolerable or relatively minor, then probably you will continue watching. And if you watch enough, those differences will disappear. The same thing happens to some of us when we first hear objectionable language in a movie. If the movie is good, we may stay even though the language offends us."

"Then when you watch enough movies of the same type," Mark concluded, "you may not be as bothered by the bad language."

"Social reality becomes defined for us," Sharon said. "We come to believe that the picture we see and hear is the type of society we live in. If XYZ is the only religious programming on television, a religious person may come to believe that we live in a society dominated by the XYZ religion."

"So if we don't want the XYZ religion to be seen as a description of social reality, perhaps even more important than our own ABC religion, we had better put on our own religious programming," Jane concluded.

"Yes, I think you could say at least that much about the influence of the media," Sharon said. "I don't mean that you'll adopt every behavior you watch. Whether you change or not depends on previously held beliefs and the strength of your values. But if our members perceive XYZ as not too different from what they believe, our denomination might lose members to XYZ."

"Just how powerful are the media?" Harold wanted to know.

"It's hard to pinpoint exactly how we are being shaped," Sharon said. "We do know that anything that constantly keeps our attention has some potential to change us. However, research on products and voting behavior shows that people still have to talk about it with someone else before they buy. I suspect the same thing is true with people changing a belief or choosing a church."

"So where does our media committee start?" asked Harold.

"You start by agreeing on a primary purpose," Sharon replied. "Are you going to use the media for marketing the church, or as a service to the community, or for ministry to your own members?"

"We want to do all three," Harriet responded. "But let's start with marketing. How do we do that?"

"First, make sure you can deliver what you offer," Sharon said. "If you advertise your church as warm and friendly, will people be greeted that way when they come?"

"I'm not so sure about that," Harold said. "I've seen visitors leave this church with only a handshake from the minister."

"Maybe we could change that by asking some of our members to serve as greeters," Bill suggested. "They could steer visitors to the refreshment table after the service so the rest of us could meet them."

Martha joined the discussion. "If people really knew our church, they wouldn't judge us just on a Sunday handshake. We do a lot of good in the community. We help disadvantaged people, the elderly, and singles, among other things."

"How would you show that to visitors?" Mark asked.

"We could take pictures and make a display in the refreshment room," Harriet said.

"Now you're getting the idea," Sharon said. "Anything you

claim in a marketing approach must at least have visual evidence to back it up."

"Our own members need to see these things too," Martha said. "It would give them a sense of cohesion as a caring community."

"The church newsletter sometimes mentions our community outreach, but maybe we need to make it a regular feature, with updates on what we are doing," Mark suggested.

Sharon smiled. "All those ideas sound right on target."

"All right, so we put something out on the shelf that people can see," Harold said. "What's next? How do we get people to come in and see what we've got?"

"If you can take photographs of your programs, why not do a series on videotape and put it on access TV?" Sharon asked.

"How much would such a project cost?" Bill wanted to know.

"The access channel is free," Harriet said. "Our only cost would be production."

"We're talking about thousands of dollars," Harold objected.

"I know one church group that did a series at very little cost," Sharon countered. "They rented some modest equipment and produced a series of four half-hour programs. Furthermore, access gave repeated airings to their tapes. I can give you some phone numbers to call to get you started. If you're interested, I also have price lists from radio stations and the newspaper."

"It seems to me we have enough information to do some follow-up work and begin making plans." Harriet beamed. "We can start with some internal marketing of our own members. I'm asking Bill to follow up on his idea of securing greeters to welcome visitors, and Martha to put together a pictorial display of our community service programs. And I want Mark to see if our church newsletter will carry a regular feature on these programs. Harold, would you check out the prices on taping for access?"

"I'll do my best," Harold replied.

"Let's see, have I left out anything?" Harriet wondered.

"That's a good beginning," Sharon said. "However, you still need to design an overall format for your community outreach campaign."

"What do you mean by 'format'?" Harriet asked.

"You need an overall layout or organizational plan that puts together a theme, an outline for your scripts, and perhaps a logo," Sharon said. "You have to consider what types of media you plan to use and how to convey your message."

"All right." Harriet laughed. "Let's ask Dr. Norris to come back for a second meeting and help us develop an overall format. We'll take a look at what we've found out and formulate a campaign plan."

Sharon Norris agreed to come back, and Harriet adjourned the meeting.

When Sharon got home, she reviewed what she had said in the meeting. She wanted to motivate the committee to use media but, at the same time, look realistically at what this actually could accomplish. A focus on "marketing" might develop some false expectations. Sharon knew that a marketing approach, especially for the church, was probably a long-range goal, with very few results in the immediate future.

The next day, Sharon decided to have lunch with Harriet and discuss her ideas about a realistic approach to a media campaign.

"I think you know the first question that should be asked about any media campaign," Sharon began. "What type of audience are you targeting?"

"You mean, Who do I want to attract? We could target unchurched adults, for example." Harriet replied.

"That's right," Sharon said. "However, a successful marketing campaign also depends on the answer to a second question: Am I offering something that my audience will value more than what others in the market are offering?"

"The answer to that is no. We're not that different from other churches, especially if we're talking about felt needs—something people value and are aware of," Harriet admitted. "But could we use the media to create a need—or at least make our audience *aware* of an unfelt need?"

"Now you're getting into an area I didn't discuss last night," Sharon said. "The two main effects of media, as I mentioned, are awareness and reinforcement. However, there are two other effects that should be mentioned. One of these addresses the issue of innovations and the possibility of creating a need. If a product is very different or novel and does not offend our values, it might capture our imagination and draw us to it."

Creating a need

Harriet was intrigued. "How does that principle apply to churches?"

"If a church using media offers a different slant on things that doesn't go against community values, it may have an impact," Sharon answered. "But it has to be something we haven't heard before that touches something fundamental in us."

"One example might be in the Bible where Jesus spoke with authority and not as the scribes and Pharisees," Harriet said, "and the people heard him gladly."

"It was something different that fit into what people understood," Sharon acknowledged.

"However, we don't want to be different from Jesus!" Harriet laughed. "How are we going to innovate when people already know about Jesus?"

"You might have a new theological emphasis that no one has thought about."

"I don't have any such revelations." Harriet leaned back in her chair. "What you are saying is that unless I have a very different message that captures the imagination and falls within cultural values, I can forget about trying to use media to create a need."

"Exactly." Sharon smiled.

"I'm glad you didn't mention this at our committee meeting." Harriet shook her head. "Our church encourages an intellectual investigation of our faith, but I doubt if we could agree on an innovative emphasis. Where does that leave us with our marketing?"

"Without the impact of a novel message, you are left with the law of repetition," Sharon replied. "Success will come, but not in a short time. You will need a multimedia approach with short repeated messages using radio, TV, and newspapers. What you can expect is community awareness of the location of the church and perhaps an image of your congregation as friendly and caring."

"I'm afraid the members of my committee will fall by the wayside if our campaign has no short-term results," Harriet said.

"Well, there are some short-range benefits in using media if you focus on something other than marketing to people outside the church," Sharon said. "You might plan your campaign in stages, with short-range objectives for each stage. For example, you've already taken the first step for marketing within the church: one member is putting together a display and another member is working with hospitality. Why not change the emphasis from greeting outsiders to one of cultivating fellowship within the church? Unless you have a well-informed congregation with a sense of community, you have a poor basis for outreach."

"All right, what's our second step?"

"Develop some programming for access TV but do it for your own congregation," Sharon said. "Don't try to impress the community with a show-biz pro-

Internal marketing

duction. Remember, access TV can be used effectively as a teleconference with members of your own group. To start out, make it simple, so that people can get used to producing for access. Do a Bible study with a soloist or a flannel-board study for children—some program with just a few participants. Later on, you can add more visuals and make your productions more interesting."

"That's a great idea!" Harriet said. "I can see people in our congregation developing a sense of community spirit just by tuning in to what others are doing."

"That's right. When people see their church doing something, it makes them feel better about themselves."

"I suppose the third step is to develop an outreach program through media," Harriet said.

"Yes, you'll want to develop a theme, perhaps a slogan, and coordinate media usage," Sharon replied. "If you plan your script carefully, the same sound track you use on your video-

External marketing

tape can be used for radio. The logo that you use on TV can be shown again in your newspaper ads. People will find it easier to identify the message of your church if you coordinate your campaign this way. More important, you are using a multimedia approach, which brings more than one sense into play. The more senses you engage, the greater the impact. Also, when you have arrived at this third stage, you have the experience gained from taking your media committee through the first two steps. You might even borrow from what we know about innovations and add novelty to your productions. Your message really doesn't have to change, but you would use a different slant in your presentation. Be sure to test innovative approaches first with your members. You don't want to turn them off."

"I'm curious about something you said a little while ago," Harriet said. "You mentioned that awareness and reinforcement are the two main effects of media. Then you said that there were two more effects also noted in media research. The impact of an innovation was one of them. What was the other?"

"Oh, your minister would be interested in this one," Sharon observed. "It's the phenomenon of *status conferral* as the result of repeated coverage on TV. When a leader appears on TV a number of times, it increases his credibility—unless the leader is in handcuffs."

Status conferral

"Well, that's an incentive for our minister to go on access TV," Harriet said. "Thank you, Sharon. You've given me a lot to think about. We'll need some dedicated members on the committee to make it work."

CONCLUSION

One of the biggest problems faced by a church media committee may be in coming to grips with a realistic picture of media influence. Even though the media have power, they will never replace the interpersonal church as an attitudinal changing force in the lives of congregational members. Television, left on eight hours a day in the average home, can create awareness, reinforcement, and a sense of social reality. However, unless the viewer talks with a friend about the product or idea and tries it out, there is usually no sale. The most important exception to this rule, which requires a substantial amount of programming, is the sense of social reality that television can create. Television's power to build on existing values and to define reality certainly justifies an ongoing media program on a regional or denominational level.

Awareness and reinforcement are necessary as first steps for influencing people, but interpersonal contact is needed to reach a final decision. If your media campaign advertises a warm, friendly congregation, your ultimate success depends on whether people discover such a congregation when they walk through the front doors of the church. On the other hand, nothing is as powerful as a multimedia campaign for creating awareness and giving the church visibility. That fact alone is cause for the church to work very hard in the use of media.

Innovative products and ideas have the best chance of catching our attention, provided the innovation does not go against our values. Therefore, it might be worth the effort to experiment with a different approach to religious programming or advertising. At the same time, if a different slant offends the existing members of our denomination, we may lose more than we gain. The wisest approach to an innovative use of media is to test-market our production on members before releasing it to the general public.

Most churches, like Harriet's, in the vignette of this chapter, will use novelty like seasoning. A little is fine; too much spoils the message. Unless the message itself is radically different from other churches, we must depend on the reinforcement of repeated messages, simply stated, over a long period of time.

As exciting as media outreach to the community can be, it is best to start the campaign with marketing within the church. There are two good reasons for making this your first step.

1. Media can develop a well-informed congregation with a sense of community spirit. This approach gives your church a stronger basis, with members equipped for witness, before you go to the final step of media outreach to the community.

2. Your members will be more tolerant of production mistakes than the general public. For example, local news on TV often has a higher percentage of viewers than the more sophisticated national news. Why? People are more interested in what happens closest to home. Local newscasters can afford to make more mistakes than national newscasters. The same principle is true with the local congregation. Your members will have a much greater appreciation of your productions than the general public, and a much higher tolerance for your mistakes. If you are new to the job of media production, the best place to start is with messages directed to your own congregation.

The remaining chapters will look carefully at each medium that you might use. One of the most exciting things that a church can do is planning for a TV production. Often the type of programming ideas you would develop for in-house (or "in-church") productions are suitable for use on access. Although the scene in the next chapter shifts to an access studio, the principles described can be used anywhere—for in-house as well as access productions.

2

Planning for TV Production

Before looking at the possible use of access television, Harold was sure of one thing: you don't get something for nothing. If cable provides free channels, he thought, there must be something in it for the cable companies. Otherwise, why would the channels be free?

Harold remembered that access involved a franchise granted to the cable company by the city. The next day, he had lunch with his friend Tim Wilson, who served on the city council when the cable company won its franchise.

"What can you tell me about access TV?" Harold asked Tim.

"I can tell you all about our access provisions in the franchise," Tim replied. "How come you're interested?"

"I'm on the media committee at my church," Harold said. "I'm supposed to report back on what, if anything, we can do on access."

Tim smiled. "You can do a lot. The city negotiated an excellent franchise agreement."

"What did you have to give away in order to get free access channels?" Harold asked skeptically.

The use of access TV

"Not a thing! It's just the other way around; it's the cable company that had to deliver. They had to outbid the other companies in order to win the franchise."

"So offering access channels is one of the ways that cable companies compete with each other." Harold was intrigued.

"That's right," Tim said. "Fortunately, we have some people on the city council who knew we could negotiate that way. One of the access channels granted in the franchise is reserved for our religious and health groups."

"You mean that *any* religious group can get on access?" Harold asked.

"They sure can," Tim answered. "The religious access channel belongs to the city, not to any one religious group. For Christians, I suspect it's like Mars' Hill, which Paul preached from in Athens—a public platform where anyone can speak."

The nature of access

"Hmm." Harold thought about how television defines social reality. "So if mainline churches don't fill the channel with programming, some way-out religious groups might do it."

"That's true. The churches will have only themselves to blame if they let others fill the channel. With our access rules, it's first come, first served."

"Is access always going to be around?" Harold asked.

"Well, our franchise is good for twelve years," Tim answered. "If the churches really make use of it, probably the city council will want to renew it. Of course, not all cable companies want access. Some of these companies are pushing for new laws that would rule out access altogether. But the more access is used by the public, the less chance access opponents have of succeeding."

"How did public access get started?" Harold asked.

"You've heard of public service announcements—PSAs—or 'broadcasting in the public interest.' " Tim did not pause for a reply. "You also know there is a government regulatory agency, the Federal Communications Commission, or FCC. For a while, the FCC required broadcast stations to produce at least some programming that benefited the public. When cable TV came along, the FCC could not require cable operators to program in the public interest because cable operators often do not originate their own programs. Basically, they provide *channels* to carry the programs of others. Cablecasting is not broadcasting. So the FCC required cable operators to provide free channels to be used by the community. That's how access was born. These free channels became known as 'access channels.' "

"So much for the history lesson," Harold quipped. "How is it done today?"

"Nowadays, in the age of deregulation and free enterprise, cable companies do not have to provide access channels unless they are negotiated in the contract—the franchise—between the community and the cable company. As I mentioned, our city negotiated an excellent franchise."

"If a city doesn't know about access until after the franchise is granted, can they renegotiate?" Harold inquired.

Tim laughed. "The city can try, but they probably won't

succeed. Once the franchise has been granted, the cable company is usually reluctant to renegotiate in favor of access."

"Is our cable company antagonistic to access?" Harold wanted to know.

"No, not so far. They have been cooperative and even encouraging of access use," Tim said. "They probably take a pro-access stance because it's good public relations."

"People are more willing to subscribe to a cable company responsive to the public," Harold guessed.

"Exactly."

Harold decided to visit the access studio provided by the cable company and see what help was available for churches. Tim had mentioned that the use of some free equipment was a part of the franchise. What Harold found was a modest-size room of about 500 square feet set aside for the access studio with a single camera and an editing station. The access coordinator, Sally Hawsley, seemed pleased to show him around and answer questions.

"Are access users allowed to take equipment out of the studio?" Harold asked.

"We have two portable cameras available for checkout after users have gone through our training," Sally replied.

"How long does the training take?"

"It takes about twenty hours to learn the basics for using the camera and the editing equipment."

"How much would you charge to do the production for us?" Harold wondered.

Sally smiled. "If the cable company produced a half-hour tape for you, it would cost several thousand dollars."

"It really pays to do it yourself!" Harold exclaimed.

"It sure does," Sally agreed, "and it's fun. You'd be surprised how many people really enjoy learning how to work the equipment. It's not that difficult."

"I guess our first production will look pretty amateurish," Harold said.

"Probably, but you'll get better with practice."

"Why would anyone watch a bunch of amateurs on access?" Harold asked.

"For the same reason you watch home movies of your children." Sally paused for a moment. "Access users have their own audiences. It's not like broadcasting for mass appeal."

"Well, I can see how our church members would enjoy watching something done at the church—even if it were less than professional," Harold said. "But that sure is a limited audience."

"That's one of the major purposes of access—to reach limited special-interest audiences," Sally explained. "I might also point out that these audiences may not be as small as you might think. Viewer surveys show that a surprising number of people do watch access because they are tired of slick, professional productions. They enjoy watching ordinary people like themselves."

"I hadn't thought about that." Harold examined the camera in the studio. "But I can see how that would be true."

"Here's something else to think about," Sally said. "Some of our users have won awards and the cable company uses their tapes on commercial channels. That's not the purpose of access, but it does happen."

"So users have something to dream about—that they can make the big time." Harold smiled. "I'm beginning to think access is a good thing for our church. It might really be exciting. Can you give us any ideas on programs?"

"I get that question all the time. Perhaps the best place to look is in the areas where your group has the most enthusiasm. When people have a real interest in a subject, that comes across on television. Another approach that might get you started is to consider the four basic formats used in TV: dramatization, documentation, visual music, and talking heads."

Program formats

Sally gave Harold a handout describing these formats.

"How will this help me with programming ideas?" Harold asked.

"I'll give you some examples from productions I've seen for religious access," Sally said. "As you can see from my handout, *dramatization* covers any production where you would use an actor to communicate religious principles. One of our access churches uses puppets to do just that in its children's show. Another church uses actors to portray parables. *Documentation* provides an in-depth coverage of a special event. We've had several churches cover their conventions using this approach. *Visual music* is a relatively new format, one example being MTV. One church youth group developed this one by using audiocassettes with favorite hymns and editing in some photographs and video footage. I remember a lot of nature shots with 'Fairest Lord Jesus.' It worked!"

"What about *talking heads?*" Harold smiled. "I bet you get more of those than you want."

"That's true," Sally said. "We do get a lot of them. All it takes is one or more persons talking on TV. However, talking heads are not necessarily bad. Some are more interesting than others—particularly if more than one head is doing the talking and visuals are used during the presentation. We have many interview shows of this sort. A lot depends on the quality of your talent."

"Some people are more boring than others."

"Yes, that's true, but you would be surprised how some people improve after watching their first performance."

"What's the secret?"

"You have to get used to the conversational style that TV requires. We have a hard time convincing ministers not to project their voice on TV as they would to a roomful of people. Also, the microphone is not hooked up to an amplifier, and you don't have to talk as slowly and distinctly as when an amplifier is used. The real secret is just being yourself. If people find you interesting in conversation, you should have no problem. In fact, a soft-spoken person may come across better on TV than in person. The director can always turn up the mike."

"Hmm." Harold thought for a moment. "Some of our lay people might do just as well as the minister."

Sally laughed. "They might be better! We'll talk some more about programming ideas when you come to my class. You'll want to consider carefully the difference between programming for access and for commercial TV."

Harold left the access studio with a new sense of mission. Before his visit, he had assumed that religious access was only a TV platform for ministers' sermons. Now he could see all sorts of people from his church appearing on access. Think of what it would mean for the children to see themselves on TV; they could do the play they put on for Bible school. The quartet from the choir that sang at family night supper would be a natural. The upcoming seminars on comparative religion taught by a philosophy professor in the church would be an excellent program to share with the community. And, yes, Harold could even see how he might fit in on access, interviewing the minister about last Sunday's sermon. The minister would come across better by casually talking about his message than by preaching it.

At the next media committee meeting, Harriet could hardly believe her ears when Harold started talking about access.

"We need to start producing for access right now," he

began. "Do you realize what it could mean to our congregation? It's not just for ministers; every member of our church has something at stake here."

Harriet laughed. "Are you going to leave out the minister?"

"No, the minister should be included. But we don't have to wait for him to get started. We can be doing things right now."

"What's the first thing we need to do?" Harriet was delighted by Harold's new enthusiasm.

"We need to get some people down to the access studio to take their training," Harold answered. "I'm going to do it myself, but I need four more to go with me."

"Why so many?" asked Bill.

"Suppose we have a production all set up and one of our trained technical people can't make it," Harold explained. "We need some backups."

"Do we have enough people with a technical background to sign up for training?" Jane inquired.

"It's not that hard," Harold said. "You don't need a technical background to learn how to use the equipment. Anybody can do it."

"Our young people would love it!" Martha joined in.

Mark frowned. "What if they break something and we have to pay for it?"

"We would still be better off not having to buy the equipment ourselves. Besides that, the equipment is not that fragile. If you think about it, some of our young people probably would be better at it than anyone here."

"I still think we need to be careful about whom we choose," Mark said.

"I'll see to it that we get responsible people," Harold insisted. "If you'll give me permission to do that, we can get started."

No one objected to Harold's offer, and the meeting concluded.

Like most new converts, Harold could not understand the lack of enthusiasm among the members of the committee for access TV. He persisted until he had recruited two high-schoolers, Jenny Barnes and Fred Wells, to take the training. He also enlisted two committee members, Mark and Jane.

To Harold's delight, Sally Hawsley arranged for a special training group for church members. As the first training session got under way, Sally talked about what it meant to do programming for access.

"I used to begin these sessions with the members of the group brainstorming for program ideas," Sally began. "The problem with that was their previous exposure to commercial television. Everyone was coming up with ideas based on what they had seen on network TV. Many of those ideas are not practical on access. We are not talking about huge productions with a thirty-member crew."

"What about just taping our worship services?" Mark asked.

"A worship service looks fine when you are actually there and participating, but it can be dull on TV," Sally said. "You need movement, interaction, and visuals in order for the viewer to feel a sense of participation."

"What do you mean?" Jane wondered.

| **Production values** |

"What I'm talking about falls under the general category of production values," Sally answered. "In order to get audience attention or create awareness, you might have to restructure your entire worship service for the TV audience. In my church, people wouldn't like those changes; it would detract from their sense of worship."

"What changes would you need?" Jane asked.

"First of all, you would need more movement than many church services provide. Even a good preacher may seem boring behind a pulpit for twenty minutes on TV. With a single speaker, you need visual inserts such as graphs, pictures, and other illustrations. You also need interaction with other people and at least some audience shots. In order to get those effects, you'd need several cameras and a lot of lighting. You don't have those resources with access equipment. Of course, some of those effects can be accomplished through editing."

"Are you saying that we have to be entertaining?" Harold wanted to know.

"Well, the number one reason that people watch TV is for entertainment," Sally reminded him.

"Entertainment is in the eye of the beholder," Mark said. "What one person considers entertainment may be boring to another."

"That's true. However, there are some general guidelines for holding the attention of a TV audience. *Motion* is one of them. That's why chase scenes will always be popular."

Jenny laughed. "How does that work in a worship service? We can't have someone chasing the preacher."

"That's my point about worship services," Sally replied.

"You are not going to get much movement unless your minister runs up and down the platform, and traditional congregations may not want that. Another thing you need for audience attention is something new and surprising. Soap operas, for example, thrive on startling new revelations—what we call 'audience grabbers.'"

"A minister might announce that the world is ending," Fred joked.

"And what would you do for an encore?"

"This discussion is getting silly," Jane said. "You don't have to go to those extremes to get people's attention. Our minister usually offers fresh insights that keep my interest."

"I didn't mean to imply that you shouldn't tape any of your worship service for access," Sally said. "A good sermon with some visuals inserted during editing might be fine. But the rest of the worship service may lack the pacing you need to hold a TV audience. Probably your best decision is to edit the service down to half an hour. The finished product could simply be some music from the choir and the sermon."

"That still might be dull," Jenny said.

"Yes, but on access you're not so concerned about mass appeal," Sally said. "You want an interesting program, but your appeal can be to a limited audience, such as your own congregation."

"I don't go to church for entertainment," Harold said. "I want to hear something that makes sense about my faith—to be better informed on how to live the Christian life. That's why I don't like most of the TV preachers I hear. All they do is jump around and recite little truisms. They offer nothing new."

"An informative program, provided that you are offering something new, is key to increased audience appeal for a growing minority of TV viewers," Sally pointed out. "They may be less interested in such entertainment values as motion, variety, and talent."

"Hmm." Mark thought for a moment. "I wonder if that's true. People might not be as receptive as you suppose. In fact, it could be argued that we are drowning in an information society. When I come home tired, I want my TV to entertain me. I get enough information at the office."

"The shows I watch are informative," Jane said. "I like public television. You can have the rest of it."

Mark changed the subject. "Sally, you mentioned something about inserting visuals. What sort of visuals do you mean?"

"You'll learn more about that in editing," Sally answered.

"When you're taping a minister with only one camera, you'll want to shoot some footage either before or after the sermon of such things as stained-glass windows, the cross, the communion table, and people in the congregation. When you do your editing, there's an insert feature that allows you to save the sound and insert visuals over the minister's voice. We'll get to that later."

"So the things we need for audience interest are movement, novelty, variety, and talent," Jenny summed up.

"That's right," Sally said. "And to some extent you can create variety with visual inserts. Also, whenever possible, it helps to have more than just one person talking. For example, instead of just taping the preacher, you might get more variety by having someone interview the minister about the sermon. You could add even more variety by putting audio excerpts from the recorded sermon into your interview."

"That's what we ought to do," Harold agreed, recognizing his own idea. "I want to do those interviews with our minister."

"I'm beginning to see how access can be made interesting." Mark paused for a moment. "We don't have to sound like TV preachers we see on the networks. The audience we are targeting is different from theirs."

"That's right." Jane nodded. "We're not into pleading for money and wowing the public with a show-biz format. But we can still use what Sally is teaching us to capture the attention of our own audience."

"What about doing a show with children?" Harold asked. "I bet that would have a strong appeal to viewers."

"If you let the children do some of the talking, it could be a real hit," Sally answered. "Unfortunately, we've had ministers who put children into the show and just preach to them. What you end up with is just another series of sermons."

"I was thinking about doing a show with our children's church school class," Harold said. "The teacher uses role play, puppets, and other techniques to involve the children."

"That sounds great for TV. I hope you do it."

"How about a program for our older people?" Fred asked. "How could you make that interesting?"

"You might start by finding an interesting older person as host—someone with warmth and a good sense of humor," Sally replied. "The host could interview one or two senior persons about their memories of the church—perhaps use some old photos or memorabilia as inserts. That sort of production would be simple and not a bad choice for beginners."

Jenny had a different idea. "I would like to see us start with the play that eight of our young people put on for the church last month."

"A play with that many performers might not work well for a one-camera production," Sally cautioned. "All the lines would be essential, so you would have a hard time editing out bad spots. You might make it work by shooting the play over again from a different angle, but I wouldn't recommend that for beginners."

"I want to see how you operate the camera," Jenny said impatiently.

Fred agreed. "Yeah, let's get to the good stuff."

"Whoa." Sally laughed. "We're still in the preproduction stage. I want you to think of yourselves as a group similar to the people you will be taping in your church. Before you let anyone near a camera, you need to know several things. The first is: What is the goal or purpose of your pro—"

Production plan

"I've got an idea," Jenny interrupted. "If we can't do the play, how about shooting the talent show we're putting on at our next fellowship dinner? No more than four people are ever on stage at once."

"All right, let's assume you're going to do that," Sally said. "The second question is: Who is the specific audience?"

"Church members and perhaps some other people we know at school," Fred answered.

"Let me give you the handout with the rest of the questions." Sally smiled as she passed out the information. "Some of the answers will be easy, but you need a clear understanding of each one. Read them over and see if you have any problems."

The class looked over the following handout:

YOUR PRODUCTION PLAN

1. What is the goal or purpose of your program?

2. Who is the specific audience?

3. What effect do you want the program to have on your audience?

4. What is the subject matter of this program and how will you use material to describe it?

5. Outline the events as they occur in the program. What is the exact sequence?

6. Which of the following programming formats will you use? Describe it briefly.

Dramatization: A play or role play with follow-up narration.

Documentation: An on-location program of an actual or staged event with voice-over narration.

Visual music: Music from an audiocassette with visual inserts.

Talking head(s): Interview, speaker with visual inserts, or a panel discussion.

A combination of the above: Describe what you will do.

"If we're doing the talent show, as Jenny suggests, most of the answers are obvious," Mark observed. "I'm not sure I understand the last part of question four, How will you use material to describe the subject matter? What material are you referring to?"

"The talent show, of course, is the subject matter," Sally replied. "The material might be props you want to include in a scene or something one of the actors is holding that's important for the audience to see."

"Give us an example," Jane said.

Sally reflected for a moment. "It could be an object you want to edit in later as a visual insert. For example, someone might be reading a scriptural passage in one of your skits."

"As a matter of fact, the talent show does open with someone reading scripture," Jenny said. "Is that especially important for production?"

"On television, people expect to see what the person is reading," Sally answered. "So you would want to make a note as to the material you are using and edit in a shot of the passage after the taping."

"Couldn't we just zoom in and do a close-up?" Fred asked.

"That probably won't work if the performer is holding the Bible," Sally responded. "A close-up would show even the slightest movement, and it would be hard for the TV audience to read the passage."

"I don't understand how you can edit in a book," Mark said.

"All you do is put the open Bible on a stand, focus the camera on the correct passage, and insert it into your finished production," Sally explained. "You would put these inserts on a separate tape after you have videotaped the talent show from start to finish."

"You mean tape over part of the picture that you've already taken?" Jane was puzzled.

"That's right. During editing, you tape over the actor reading the Bible by inserting a close-up of the passage itself."

"Won't you also erase the actor's voice?" Harold inquired.

"No, the audio is on a separate part of the tape," Sally explained. "In this case, you only erase the video and put in a new picture."

"Wow!" Jenny exclaimed. "If we can erase one picture and put in another, then we need to look at what we are doing in the talent show and think about other inserts."

"That's what I meant by using materials to describe your subject matter," Sally said. "You can do that with anything you want your audience to focus on—an object, a scripture passage, a book title, or even a reaction shot of another actor."

"One of our scenes has an actor holding a flower," Fred said. "Should we edit in a close-up?"

Production log

"You might, if the flower has some special meaning in the skit. Keep track of whatever material you decide to use. Don't just mark it down in the script, write it into your production log."

"Production log?" Harold repeated.

"A log is a short record showing where you will use your material," Sally answered. "For example, if the clock or counter shows you are twenty minutes into your taping when the actor holds up the rose, note the time and the material you want to insert. Otherwise, you will spend all day looking through the tape and trying to find your edits."

"I feel dumb," Mark said. "I don't understand how you put pictures on a tape or how you do edits or any of this."

Sally laughed. "You'll understand a lot more when we get into editing. But you can see the need to discuss a production before you do it. That's what the production plan is for. Some questions will be more important than others, depending on the sort of things you will be doing in your programming format. The concerns you have in taping a talent show are going to be different from the production of an interview or a visual music show. The production plan is a checklist to make sure you have covered the main questions about whatever you are producing. In our next class, we'll learn how the camera works."

CONCLUSION

Access agreements differ from community to community. What access provides for all communities, within the franchise agreement between the community and the cable company, are free channels that can be used for community interests.

Sometimes the free use of production equipment, along with free training, also is negotiated. The channel itself is the most valuable part of access; the commercial leasing of a channel can require a five-digit figure per month.

Programming for access is very different from programming for a commercial channel. Access can be used effectively as a teleconference or a morale builder for an audience no larger than your own congregation, or it can be used to reach the entire community. Viewers watch access because it features ordinary people like themselves, people they often know personally.

Access and commercial television carry the same requirements for gaining audience attention: novelty, motion, variety, and talent. In other words, audience interest increases with the showing of visuals, a variety of people (two or more), movement in the scenes or the actors (something besides a stony face addressing the camera), the offering of something new with a fresh perspective, and talent with an appealing personality and a relaxed conversational style. Not all these qualities may be possible at once, but a program without any of these features is dull.

Production values is a broad term used to describe the appeal of a production and includes lighting, sound, camera work, and editing as well as the audience interest values just mentioned. Access has one big advantage over commercial TV in gaining audience interest—the novelty of seeing people you know on TV.

A script may not be needed (especially in talk shows), but a *production plan* with a sequence of events or outline is necessary (see example in chapter 9). Otherwise, your production will take on a home-movie appearance, with the camera trailing the action. Much of TV production is anticipation of *what* shots should be taken *when.*

Harold Jordan and the other members in training are learning how to produce for TV one step at a time. As you listen to the class discussion in the next chapters, you will become familiar with the basic concepts of production. At the very least, you will know what resource people to seek out in the community for further assistance. Also, you will know what is happening in a TV studio and, should you get into production, the equipment will be familiar.

3

"Lights, Camera, Action!"

Harold was delighted when no one else showed up to attend the access studio's special training program for churches except the members of his own group. With Sally all to themselves, they could ask whatever questions they wanted.

"Let's begin with a discussion of how the camera works with light," Sally said.

"That's easy," Fred said confidently. "TV cameras use pickup tubes to receive the light. When the light strikes a pickup tube, a small electrical current is produced in the tube."

"Very good," Sally said. "The camera we are using has three pickup tubes, one for each primary color: red, blue, and green. You mix them together and get white." (See Figure 3-1.)

"Why is that important?" Jane wanted to know.

"Well, there's a switch labeled WHITE BALANCE on the cam-

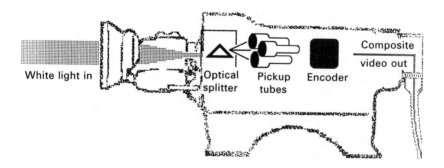

Figure 3-1. Diagram of 3-tube camera.
Light enters the camera through the lens, is focused into the optical system which splits the light into red, green, and blue components, then onto the surface of each pickup tube. The current from each pickup tube is processed in the encoder, which then combines the various signals into composite video.

era that's used for balancing the color," Sally replied. "You focus the camera on a white object and push the switch."

"What happens if you forget to do the white balance?" Mark asked.

Setting the white balance

Sally laughed. "You will probably produce a show with green people. So after you have turned on the camera and let it warm up for ten minutes or so you should adjust the white balance. That way you get equal parts of red, blue, and green. Presto! White light!"

"Is that procedure the same for indoors and outdoors?" Fred asked.

"Yes, except for one thing. There's a color correction filter you'll need to set. On most cameras you turn a little filter dial that indicates the type of lighting you want, indoor or outdoor.

Setting the filter

The filters are colored plastic gels built between the lens and the pickup tubes. They filter out certain frequencies of light."

"Some cameras have only one pickup tube," Fred said. "Are they treated the same way?"

"Exactly," Sally replied. "You set the filter and the white balance the same as you would with a three-tube camera. This same procedure works with solid-state chip cameras."

"Which is the better camera, three-tube or one-tube?" Jane inquired.

"Most three-tube or three-chip cameras give you better color and resolution."

"What's 'resolution'?" Mark asked.

"Resolution has to do with how many lines the camera produces to form a picture," Sally said. "The more lines, the better your picture is defined."

"How often do you have to adjust the white balance?" Jenny asked.

"Every time you change the quality of light, you need to check the white balance again. For example, what is white indoors will be light blue outdoors because sunlight has more blue in it than artificial light. So you need to reset the white balance. You'd be surprised how many people forget to make these adjustments and end up with poor productions."

"Let's get to the zoom and the focus," Fred said eagerly.

"Why don't you tell us the difference between the two?" Sally suggested.

"All right." Fred took up the challenge. "The zoom takes you closer or farther away from the subject, sort of like a telescope.

The focus is something you adjust to get a sharper picture."

"Right. Another way to look at it is that the zoom controls what light will be directed to the pickup tubes," Sally continued. "Sometimes the lighting will be fine for close-ups, but when you zoom out for a wider picture, you'll discover the lighting is inadequate. When you are taping, you can see that happening on your monitor or the TV set you have hooked up to your recorder."

Using the zoom

"You mean you can see what's happening as you shoot it?" Harold asked.

"Yes. In fact you can use your monitor or TV set before you start taping," Sally answered. "You can tell a lot about your lighting just by experimenting with different shots before the production. If your lighting is poor on certain shots, you can readjust your lamps, if you are indoors, or move out of the shade, if you are outdoors."

"Where's the zoom located?" Jane asked.

"The zoom control is found either on top of the lens itself or on the right handle of a studio tripod," Sally replied. "On our camera, there's a switch on top of the lens that rocks back and forth, so it's called a rocker switch." (See Figure 3-2.)

"Where's the focus?" Harold wondered.

"On most cameras, such as ours, the focus is the outermost ring on the lens. On a studio camera, the focus can be set by turning the left handle of the tripod."

"When you refer to the lens, you mean the part that sticks out front with the glass on the end?" Jane asked.

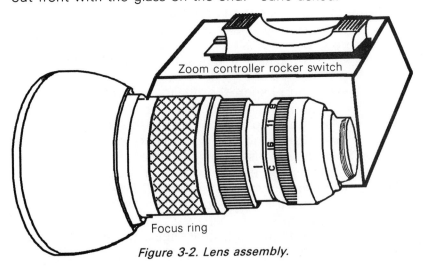

Figure 3-2. Lens assembly.

"Right. The focus ring is next to the glass part," Sally replied. "You turn the ring until the picture is sharply in focus. It's important to know how to set the focus before you start tap-

Presetting the focus

ing. All you have to do is to zoom in as close as you can on the subject and set the focus. This sets the lens's depth of field, or how much of the area is in focus, between your camera and your subject. From there on you can zoom in or zoom out; you don't need to reset the focus."

"So you preset the focus on a close-up?" Fred asked.

"That's right. You only have to set it once and the camera stays in focus, whether you go for a wide shot or a close-up. Of course, you'll need to reset the focus if your subject moves away from you or if you zoom in tight on another subject a different distance away. The tighter or closer the shot, the more critical the focus becomes."

"In other words, the picture is most likely to be fuzzy when you go in close," Jenny concluded.

"Yes, but if you've preset your focus, you won't have that problem. Only when you change to a different subject a different distance away do you reset it."

"What about the f-stop? Do we have to set it?" Fred asked.

"What's an f-stop?" Mark inquired.

"The f-stop controls how much light gets into the camera. It's the iris ring right behind the focus ring," Sally said. "Almost all video cameras have an automatic iris control, which senses the proper amount of light and sets the iris accordingly." (See Figure 3-3.)

"The iris ring sets the f-stop?" Harold asked.

"Yes. Leave the automatic switch on, Fred, and don't worry about it—with one exception," Sally said. "When you have a background object that is brighter than your subject, the auto

When to adjust the iris

iris will set itself on the brighter object."

"And your subject will be too dark." Jenny had experience with f-stops from her own 35mm camera. "So you need to switch the auto iris off and turn the iris ring to let in more light. In f-stop language, you open the iris by turning to a lower f-stop."

"Exactly, but with one word of caution," Sally noted. "You can overload your pickup tubes with more light than they can handle. You have to be careful not to let too much in. If your brighter objects in the picture start to glow in the monitor or viewfinder, you'll know to readjust the iris."

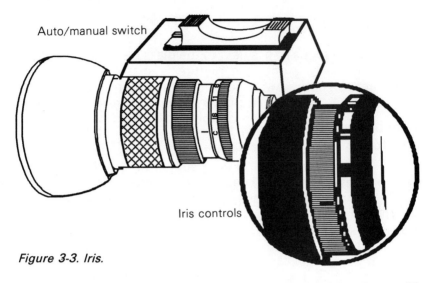

Auto/manual switch

Iris controls

Figure 3-3. Iris.

"Can you damage the camera by pointing it into the sun?" Mark asked.

"You certainly can!" Sally said. "The same thing goes for pointing the camera at any bright light—don't do it, not even when the camera is off. You can also damage the camera by dropping it, or by putting it in the trunk of a car and driving on a rough road, or by failing to protect it from rain or water. There's a little picture hanging over my desk as a reminder of those no-no's. Otherwise, your camera is fairly durable and you shouldn't be afraid to handle it." (See Figure 3-4.)

Camera safety

"All right, so far we've learned about camera safety, the filter, white balancing, the zoom, the focus, and the iris," Harold summarized. "What's next?"

"Next we need to look at our camera setup and see how it's hooked up to the recorder." Sally walked toward the camera. "Certain connections, such as the camera cable that runs from the camera to the recorder, are made a little differently from others. They may plug in with a connector that has pins on the end of it or they may twist on in the way you would connect a cable to your television set at home."

The class studied the hookups and practiced attaching cords to the equipment. (See Figure 3-5.)

"We have a small color TV, a monitor, hooked up to the recorder so that we can tell something about the color and the lighting," Sally continued. "Of course, you can also see a black-and-white picture on the viewfinder of the camera."

"Why not just watch the picture on the monitor and forget the viewfinder?" Fred asked.

"The viewfinder is the most accurate way of framing your shots," Sally replied. "The color monitor helps with the lighting and the color, but that's only an indicator. The colors will differ from one monitor to another. You can be fooled into thinking you don't need to white-balance when you do. You should always white-balance regardless of how the colors look on the monitor.

"Let's try some practice shots."

"Now we're getting to the fun part," Jenny said as she and Fred walked over to the camera. "How do you turn this thing on?"

Figure 3-4. Camera safety rules.

Never aim a camera at the sun or any bright light.
Do not let the camera get wet.
Do not drop or treat a camera roughly.

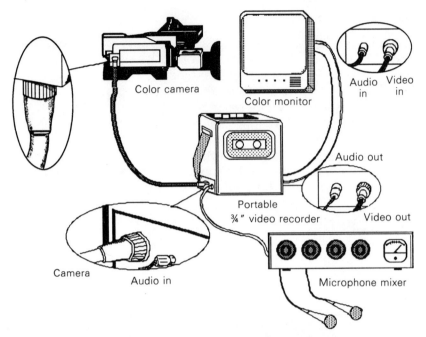

Figure 3-5. Camera hooked up to equipment.

"The switch is located on the power pack—that metal box on the floor," Sally told her. "Turn it on and tell me what you do next."

"Next I look for the filter, which must be this little dial with the numbers on it. It says on the side of the camera that number one is for quartz lighting." Jenny looked at the overhead spotlights. "Is that what we are using?"

"That's right—so turn the dial to number one." (See Figure 3-6.)

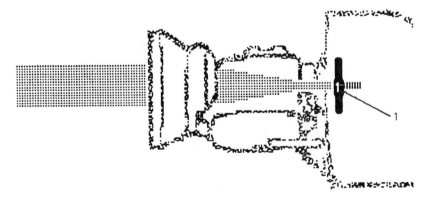

Figure 3-6. Filter wheel.

"Then we set the white balance," Fred said. "Here's the switch. What do I do next?"

"Have someone walk over to the stage, where the lighting will be on the talent, and hold up something white," Sally answered.

Harold stood on the platform of the set and held up a piece of white paper.

"Now I find the rocker switch on top of the lens and zoom in for a close-up of the paper," Fred continued. "Now what?"

"Turn the focus ring until you get a sharp image of the paper," Sally responded. "Then push the white-balance switch down, hold it for a couple of seconds, and release it."

"That sounds simple enough," Mark said.

"Oops! We forgot to turn on the spotlights." Sally laughed. "You'll have to do the white balance again because the lighting will be different."

This time Mark set the white balance.

"Now are we ready to shoot?" Harold asked.

"All set," Sally replied. "We need an interviewer and an interviewee to take their places on the platform."

"Why do we need a platform?"

"It gives a better angle for the camera. You can shoot straight at the subjects."

Jane took Harold by the arm and led him over to the stage. "Harold and I will do the interview," she said. "We'll clip on these mikes by the chairs."

"Fine," Sally told her. "But don't put your mike too close to your necklace, Jane; it'll make a rattling sound. Clip it on a little higher up—about six inches away from your chin on the side you'll be talking to Harold."

"What's this little box with the mike cords running to it?" Mark asked.

"That's called a mixer," Sally said. "Incidentally, those mike cords also are called audio cables. How about acting as our sound person?"

"What have I got to do?"

"Nothing much." Sally smiled. "Look at these little control knobs on the mixer. Harold's audio cable runs into knob number one and Jane's is knob number two. You look at the meter on the mixer and adjust the sound so that the needle goes up to the red but not in it." (See Figure 3-7.)

Adjusting the audio

"I adjust the sound for each mike by turning its knob up or

down." Mark looked at the numbers on the knobs. "Each knob has to be adjusted separately."

"Probably you'll have to turn Harold down and Jane up," Sally said. "That's all there is to it." She went over to the recorder, which was located a few feet away from the camera.

Using the recorder

"We'll let Jenny operate the camera first, and Fred will operate the recorder."

"Does this recorder work the same way as my home recorder?" Fred asked.

"Just about," Sally replied. "Push the EJECT button and put in the tape; then push PLAY and RECORD together when you are ready to tape. We'll let you trade places with Jenny on the camera after a few minutes."

Jenny was looking through the viewfinder at Jane and Harold. "On which subject do I preset my focus?"

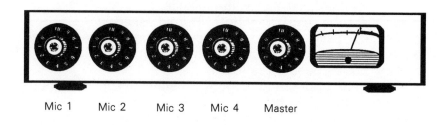

Mic 1   Mic 2   Mic 3   Mic 4   Master

Figure 3-7. Audio knobs and meter.

"They're both about the same distance from the camera," Sally replied, "so it doesn't matter. Zoom in on one of them as tight as you can get, then turn the focus ring on the front of the lens."

"All right, I've got Harold's face as close as I can go." Jenny turned the focus ring. "The picture looks sharp."

"Now you can leave the focus alone and concentrate on your shots," Sally said. "You start off with an establishing shot of the scene. In this case, it's a two-shot of Harold and Jane."

(See Figure 3-8.)

Composing the shots

"What do I do next?"

"Since Jane is interviewing Harold, you would take a slow zoom from your two-shot to a medium or waist shot of Jane," Sally said. (See Figure 3-9.) "Then, when Harold starts talking, you would take a slow zoom-out and go back to your two-

Figure 3-8.
Visual of two-shot.

shot," Sally continued. "If you think Harold is going to talk for a while, go in on a slow zoom and take a medium shot of him."

"How slow should I do my zooms?" Jenny asked.

"Use a very light touch on the rocker switch and go as slowly as you can without pausing in between. It takes practice to do a good zoom, so don't expect to get it perfect the first time."

"I get the idea." Jenny practiced with the zoom. "I go from a two-shot to a medium shot, back out to a two-shot, and then to a medium."

"Well, if they are both talking back and forth with neither dominating the conversation, you should hold your two-shot," Sally cautioned. "Otherwise you'll have your audience seasick from too much zooming in and out."

"What are these little knobs on the tripod?" asked Jenny.

Figure 3-9.
Visual of medium
shot.

"I was coming to that. Those knobs allow you to move the camera itself. The side knob is called the tilt knob. It releases the tension so the camera can tilt up and down. Once you've done that, the camera can swing up or down, so don't let go of it." (See Figure 3-10.)

Adjusting the tilt knob

"When would I need to use the tilt knob?" Jenny loosened the tilt knob so that the camera moved freely up and down.

"You often have to adjust for headroom of the subjects you have in the picture. For example, let me show you a shot of Harold with too much headroom." (See Figure 3-11.)

"To correct that picture, you would tilt the camera down until there is just a little space between the top of Harold's head and the top of the frame. Here's how it should look." (See Figure 3-12.)

"And if I went too far down and cut off part of Harold's head, I would tilt up," Jenny concluded.

"Right. If a director was telling you what to do, the command would be 'tilt up' or 'tilt down.' "

"What's this other knob in front of me?" Jenny wanted to know. (See Figure 3-13.)

Adjusting the pan knob

"That's the knob that lets you pan—move the camera from left to right," Sally responded. "It's a good idea to loosen the pan knob slightly so you will always be prepared to 'pan left' or 'pan right.' " (See Figure 3-14.)

The rest of the class time was spent with each person gaining experience on each piece of equipment. Sally watched the

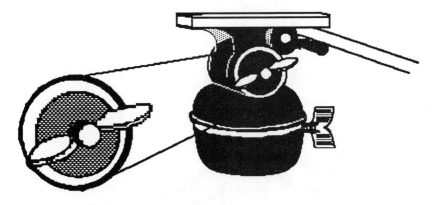

Figure 3-10. Tilt knob.

monitor and occasionally called out such camera commands as "Pan right" or "Pan left," to center the picture from left to right, or "Tilt up" or "Tilt down," to allow for proper headroom. Sometimes she would say "Check your focus," "Hold your two-shot," or "Keep your zoom slow and steady." The members of the class soon got the idea and their confidence increased. Sally also handed out a step-by step summary as a checklist and reminder.

Figure 3-11. Too much headroom.

   1. Turn on camera; let it warm up for about ten minutes.
   2. Turn on lighting. Adjust for white balance with someone on stage holding up white card or paper.
   3. Loosen pan and tilt knobs (retighten tilt knob before you let go of the camera).
   4. Turn on audio mixer and do a mike check on each performer (turn other mikes down).

Figure 3-12. Proper amount of headroom.

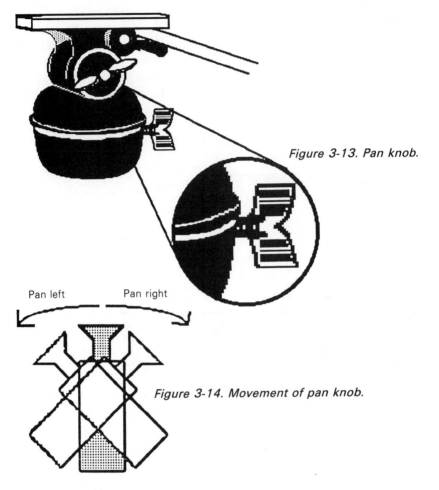

Figure 3-13. Pan knob.

Pan left   Pan right

Figure 3-14. Movement of pan knob.

5. Preset focus, using most extreme close-up of subject farthest away.

6. Turn on recorder when you are ready to begin taping.

At the end of the class, Fred and Jenny announced that they were ready to organize the production crew for an on-location shoot of the talent show. Sally said producing the talent show would be a good way to get into editing, and they agreed on a time to do it.

CONCLUSION

Certainly there is a difference between taping a small production with modest equipment and a large production with a control booth and a multicamera system. The advantages of a larger system will be explored in the next chapter. However, the authors started out in a small studio with a single camera and trained over a hundred church members in its use. Single-camera productions often are worthy of access and are thoroughly enjoyed by the congregation during in-house use. Also, starting with a simple system allows the user to add other equipment later.

Learning the basic functions and terminology of TV production can present some readers with information overload. However, once you get into TV programming, you will want to reread these sections on production. Learning production terminology is useful not only for those behind the camera but also for the talent in front of the camera. Otherwise, discussing production goals is difficult.

The term "production" as it applies to television usually refers to the recording of the actual event by the camera. (Sometimes it is used in the generic sense for anything that goes on in a TV studio.) "Post-production," which is also covered in the next chapter, refers to editing. The mistakes made in production become very clear in post-production, as the class members will soon find out.

4

Making the Production Look Better

Jenny and Fred, the two teenage members of the media committee, were successful in getting the youth group together and videotaping their church talent show on location. After the taping, the production class got together for their first editing lesson. Sally knew the group would have a keen interest in editing their own production. However, she also knew that beginners typically run into problems. She did not want them to become discouraged.

"You took on a fairly complex project for your first production," Sally began, "but I think this experience will be a valuable lesson. Certainly you will see a variety of problems."

"I didn't see anything so hard about producing the talent show," Jenny objected. "We had a good time."

Sally smiled. "Let's take a look at the tape. I want you to watch the raw footage and take notes of anything you don't like, such as camera angle or sound."

"What do you mean by 'raw footage'?" Mark asked.

"It's like the first draft of a manuscript, the unedited version," Sally replied. "You should look at what you got with the camera and make some notes before you begin editing."

As the class watched their unedited production, they were both embarrassed and disappointed. Jenny sounded heartbroken.

"We can't show that on TV," she said sadly. "It looks like home movies."

"Let's pinpoint some of the things you didn't like," Sally said. "What about the camera work?"

"That was my job and I blew it!" Jenny confessed. "All that zooming in and out. It makes you seasick to watch it."

"All right, we'll edit out some of those zooms," Sally responded. "Anything else?"

"The sound was bad," Fred said.

"Where did you have the mike?" Sally asked.

"We used the mike on top of the camera," Jane replied.

"I should have warned you about that before," Sally said. "Normally, the mike or mikes should be placed close to the performers. The only time you should attach a mike to the camera is when you are shooting one person a few feet away."

"Can editing correct the sound?" Mark asked.

"Only in a very limited way," Sally answered. "We can ride the volume controls during the editing and adjust the sound up or down. However, there's an increased hissing whenever you turn the volume up. You'll hear the lines better, but the sound will not be as distinct as you would like."

"The thing that bothered me most," Harold observed, "was that the camera often seemed to be trailing the action. That's what gave it a home-movie appearance."

"If you don't have a script," Sally said, "the only way to anticipate shots in a skit or a drama is to look through the camera viewfinder ahead of time, during rehearsal, and make notes as to what happens when."

"There was no way to do that," Jenny told her. "The participants rehearsed their skits at home."

"Well, in that case the only thing you can do is follow standard procedures: start with a wide shot to establish what is going on; then move in closer as the action begins. The climax of the scene is usually played in close up."

"In other words, I shouldn't have kept going back out to wide shots," Jenny said. "But isn't that what you taught us to do in the interview situation?"

"A wide shot in a two-person interview will still let you see faces," Sally pointed out. "Television is faces—that's what the viewing audience wants to see. A wide shot of four persons in a skit will establish the scene but it won't show faces. Unless all four people are actively involved, you should try for two-shots once the action begins."

"That's hard to do when you don't know what's going to happen when," Fred said.

"True," Sally conceded. "A production without a production plan or a rehearsal session is at a real disadvantage. Let's get into editing. After you learn the basics, we'll turn on the equipment and see what we can salvage from your production. Certainly you will like your edited version better than your raw footage."

Sally passed around a handout entitled *Basics of Editing*. The class stared at the unfamiliar language of the first section.

   I. Components
      A. Video information (one channel)
         Recording a video signal (picture), if continuous, produces a *control track*. The control track divides the video signal into 30 frames per second and sets the timing pulses for editing.
      B. Audio information (two channels)
         Recording an audio signal (sound) does *not* produce a control track. The audio uses the control track from the video to time its edits.

"I find your technical jargon disconcerting," Mark announced. "How are we ever going to learn this stuff?"

"Relax," Sally said. "I've never lost a student yet. The first thing you need to understand is that editing a videotape is done electronically. You

| **Components** |

don't need a pair of scissors and Scotch tape. You look at two television screens or monitors and transfer information from one tape to the other by pushing a couple of buttons. What makes this process possible is the control track that you lay down on the tape."

"What's a control track?" asked Harold.

"It's a continuous video signal," Sally said, "or any unbroken video picture that you record onto the tape."

"So we automatically laid down a control track when we recorded the talent show?" Fred

| **Control track** |

guessed.

"Yes. The signal remains unbroken until you stop the camera and start again," Sally answered.

"Uh-oh, what happens when we start and stop again?" Fred remembered stopping the camera and starting again during the talent show.

"Then you get a glitch," Sally replied. "The same burst of light you get from a blank tape. You've seen what a blank tape looks like from your VCR at home."

"It's a static-looking light with black dots," Fred said. "Some people call it snow. There's one of those on our raw footage."

"Right. The glitch, or snow, means no control track," Sally continued. "When a glitch occurs, then the control unit of the editor, the controller, has no signal to grab onto and make an edit—at least not in that spot. Later you'll see how the controller coordinates both the player and the recorder by remote control and allows you to set your edits."

Mark frowned. "I'm having a hard time visualizing the control track."

"Think of it as a train track being laid out," Sally said. "As long as there is a continuous track, the train has no problem."

"The control track is a continuous picture recorded by the camera or another recorder," Jenny concluded.

"Right," Sally said. "Any continuous picture will do. Sometimes, when you are working in a studio, you will close the lens of the camera and just record a black picture. When you lay down your control track this way, it's called 'laying on black.'"

"Why would you want to do that?" Jenny asked.

"There are a number of reasons," Sally replied. "Remember, you're working with at least two tapes in editing. You have the tape you produced with your raw footage, and the master on which you will make your final edits. Sometimes it's easier to work with a master that has a control track of black already recorded. For example, you may need to reserve some black at the beginning of a program so you can go back and insert titles."

"This handout mentions audio information on two channels," Harold remarked. "What does that mean?"

"We have that capability with the three-quarter-inch tapes we'll be using," Sally answered. "What it means is that you can record voices on one audio track and dub in music or whatever you want on the other."

Audio tracks

"I think my train just jumped the track," Mark quipped. "What you're talking about is a track with three layers—one for video and two for audio. That sounds more like a club sandwich than a railroad."

Sally laughed. "That's right. The channels are very much like layers in a sandwich. You can lay them on one at a time or all together. Here's a picture illustrating how they function on a tape." (See Figure 4-1.)

"Do the audio tracks have anything to do with the control track?" Fred wondered.

"No, the audio signal will not produce a control track," Sally replied. "But you do need a video control track before you can edit in the audio. Let's look at the next point in the handout. You have a choice between two types of edits."

The class looked carefully at point II of the handout:

II. Types of edits
   A. Assemble editing
      1. All information laid down at once (think of laying brand-new train track with train on it).
      2. Edits start cleanly and end with band of snow (no control track).
   B. Insert editing
      1. Use previous control track; must be unbroken.
      2. Can be any combination of video and audio tracks.
      4. Edits start cleanly and end cleanly (think of it as train cars on previously laid track).

"Let's look at the controller and see how easy editing really is," Sally said. "Look at these four little buttons."

The class looked at the buttons on the controller. (See Figure 4-2.)

Types of edits

"After you turn on the controller, you can select any of these four buttons, depending on what you want to do," Sally said. "Notice that there is only one button for Assemble editing. The Assemble mode will *not* let you select between the video and audio channels. It's all or nothing."

"So all the information goes down at once when you choose Assemble," Jenny concluded. "When would you want to use Assemble?"

"Suppose you have three segments that you want to add one right after the other," Sally replied, "and the master tape is blank, with no control track. What the Assemble edit does

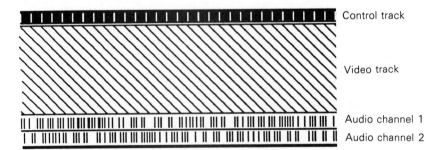

Figure 4-1. Video and audio tracks.

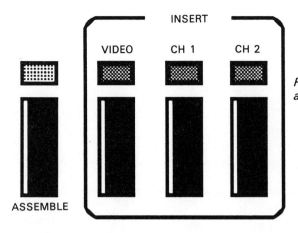

Figure 4-2. Assemble and insert buttons.

is to tie one set of pictures on to another while laying down the control track at the same time. It works like tying strings together from end to end."

"So the Assemble edit lays down a series of pictures that produces a control track," Fred said. "At the end, you tack on yet another series and then another. Can you go back and use Assemble to insert a picture in the middle?"

"Never!" Sally exclaimed.

"Why are you so emphatic about it?" Mark wanted to know.

"Because if you try to do an insert in the Assemble mode, you will replace all your recorded information—video, audio, and control track—and leave a glitch at the end," Sally warned. "Not only does the glitch look bad but the tape becomes unplayable over the air."

"What can you do to correct it?" Jane asked.

"You have to reedit the entire tape," Sally replied. "Trying to do an insert in the Assemble mode is a common mistake that costs a couple of hours to correct."

"So if you want to insert a picture, you have to push the VIDEO INSERT button," Harold said.

"Correct. But the insert button can be used only when you have a previously recorded control track."

"So that's how you erase one picture and put in another," Fred said. "You use the insert button."

"Yes, you can insert two separate audio recordings and one video recording," Sally answered. "Let's take a look at the next point of the outline. It shows the machines used in editing."

III. Editing equipment
    A. Editing controller
        Remote control for videotape machines.

B. Player (sometimes referred to as the "source" machine)
Plays raw footage to be transferred to master.
C. Editing recorder
Receives signals to be edited from the player.

The class looked at the total configuration of the editing equipment. (See Figure 4-3.)

"So the player has its television screen, or monitor, and the recorder has one too," Jane observed. "You

Editing equipment

can see the raw footage on the player's screen and the edits taking place on the recorder's."

"That's all there is to it," Sally said. "We're ready for the next point on the handout."

IV. Performing the edit
A. Operator selects point on raw footage where edit will begin (search dials allow operator to find information quickly on tape with the help of a counter).
B. Once edit points are found, operator enters the entry point at the place where the edit should occur. The controller unit "remembers" the point on the tape.
C. Operator repeats procedure on master tape in the editing recorder.
D. Operator previews the edit to see if edit points are correct.
E. Operator either resets the edit points or actually makes the edit onto the master tape.

"I'm lost," Mark complained.

"It's not that hard," Sally said reassuringly. "All that's involved is just a few buttons on the controller. The search dials are those round knobs and the entry buttons

Performing the edit

are right above them."

The class took another look at the controller. (See Figure 4-4.)

"Hmm." Fred studied the buttons. "I see entry buttons IN and OUT, for both the player and the recorder. I leap to the conclusion that 'in' means the point where you begin the edit and 'out' is where you end it."

Sally laughed. "A brilliant deduction."

"So the controller sets the edit points by remote control for both the player and the recorder," Fred said. "You also have two remote-control search dials, one for the player and one for the recorder. How does all that work?"

"That's something that becomes clearer in practice," Sally

Figure 4-3. Editing equipment and monitors.

said. "As an example, suppose you are doing an insert. You would first find the raw footage, the cutaway, that you want to insert from the player. You use the search dial on the player side of the controller to advance the tape. Then you watch the monitor to find the point where you want to begin the edit. Next you push the IN button on the player side to enter that spot into memory."

"Oh, now I see," Fred said. "Then I would go to the search dial on the recorder side of the controller and find the place

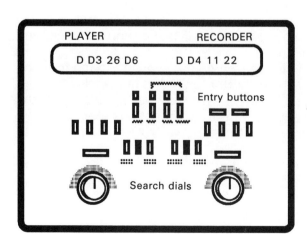

*Figure 4-4.
Editing controller.*

where I want the edited material to go in. But what about the OUT button for ending the edit? Do I enter that for the player or the recorder or both?"

"Well, you can only select one out point," Sally replied. "Your choice depends on where you want to end the edit. For example, suppose you had videotaped a person reading the Bible and wanted to insert a picture of the scripture passage. You have the scripture passage on the player and the person reading the Bible on the recorder. You would end the edit on the recorder at the point where the person finishes reading the scripture."

"Let me see if I understand that," Jenny said. "You would time the insert on the recorder so that the scripture is inserted during the reading. The edit would show the person starting to read the Bible, then the picture of the scripture would come on, and you would end the insert by showing the person finishing the reading."

"I think we should get more of our teenagers involved in production," Mark whispered to Harold. "They catch on faster than we do."

"Tell us about the PREVIEW button," Jane requested.

"That button has saved me more grief than any other feature on the controller," Sally replied. "When you've set your edit points, all you do is push the PREVIEW button and you can see exactly what you would get on the monitor."

"Without recording it?" Harold asked.

Sally smiled. "Yes, that's the beauty of the PREVIEW button. You can see what you are getting before actually recording it. Then, if you like what you see, you can press the EDIT button and do the recording. Since the edit points were entered into memory, the machine takes care of finding the spot and you don't need to rewind."

"Will the PREVIEW button warn you if you are trying to do an insert with the ASSEMBLE button on?" Jenny asked.

"No, not on this equipment," Sally replied. "That's one of the reasons why so many operators make that mistake. You have to keep your fingers away from the ASSEMBLE button when you are doing inserts.

"Let's look at the final point of the handout for some other common editing mistakes."

V. Common editing mistakes
   A. Assemble edit in the middle of a program.
   B. Not enough or broken control track in program.

C. Skipping preview steps.
D. Poor balance between the two audio channels.
E. Lack of consistent video or audio levels between edited sections.
F. Putting two similar shots together (jump cuts).

"I have a couple of questions about the last two points," Mark said. "First, tell us how you control the video levels."

"It's this little knob on the recorder," Sally replied. "It controls the intensity of the color. You watch the

Common mistakes needle in the Vu-meter just as you do with the audio. You should make sure that the readings are the same from one edit to the next and adjust them accordingly." (See Figure 4-5.)

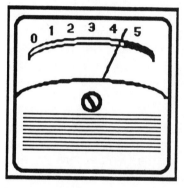

Figure 4-5. Video level knob and meter.

VIDEO LEVEL

"All right," Mark replied. "Now tell us what you mean by 'jump cuts.'"

"A jump cut is a typical rookie mistake," Sally answered. "I can best describe it by giving you an example. For instance, if you are editing an interview show that went too long, you would try to find a part that was not essential to the program and edit it out. If you begin your edit with a profile shot of the host, don't try to match the end of your edit with another profile shot at that same angle. Choose a picture with a different angle, or, better yet, end the edit with a picture of the guest. Otherwise, you will produce a jump cut that makes the host jump around as if in a silent movie."

The rest of the class time was spent in editing the talent show. At one point, they came to a glitch, where the camera was stopped and started again.

"What happened here?" asked Sally.

"The circuit breaker tripped," Fred replied. "We had two lights plugged into a twenty-amp circuit. Next time we'll check out what outlets are hooked up to what circuits."

"Good idea." Sally laughed. "Preparation is the key to any type of production. Lights, sound, camera—everything should be hooked up and tested before the production starts."

Sally was able to edit out the section around the glitch. Soon the class was doing the edits themselves, putting the entire production together on ASSEMBLE and then going back on IN-SERT to include the cutaways they had recorded on another tape. The final product was so decided an improvement over the original footage that the next Sunday their minister proudly announced the air date of the talent show on the access channel.

Fred and Jenny were still interested in producing the play performed by the youth group. They had heard that the media people at Parkway Church, a few blocks away, had developed

Two-camera system

their own studio with a two-camera system, so they made an appointment with the volunteer youth director, Joanne Blackwell, for a tour of the studio. Joanne also was trained as one of the studio's technical directors.

"Wow," said Jenny as she looked over the studio. "You really have a nice setup here."

"You should have seen this room before we fixed it up," Joanne said. "It was just an old unused classroom. We painted the walls a medium blue and hung up a movable gold curtain to make it camera-friendly. The little room next to it was made into a control room."

Fred looked at the machines. "I don't understand the equipment in your control room or how it works."

"Well, you said you've worked with a camera and a recorder," Joanne replied. "All the equipment here fits in the middle of that same system. Look at the diagram on the wall and you'll see what I mean."

Fred and Jenny looked at a simple chart:

CAMERA

↓

CCU (remote control unit for camera)

↓

SWITCHER (special effects generator)

↓

GRAPHICS (character generator)

↓

RECORDER (editing recorder)

"This looks like a flow chart," Jenny said.

"That's what it is." Joanne pointed to the word CAMERA. "Everything flows downstream from the camera to the recorder."

"So the camera is hooked up to the CCU and the CCU to the switcher, and on down to the recorder," Fred concluded. "How does the CCU work?"

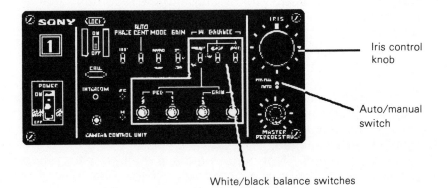

Figure 4-6. Camera control unit.

"CCU stands for 'camera control unit.' It operates some of the camera's functions by remote control," Joanne answered. "For example, this little dial sets the iris, and the switch next to it sets the white balance." (See Figure 4-6.)

"So the director sitting in the control room makes most of

the camera adjustments." Jenny looked at the equipment. "Actually, you have two CCUs, one for each camera."

"Tell us about the switcher." Fred looked at the array of buttons. "I suppose that's what you use to switch back and forth from one camera to the other."

"This particular switcher does more than that," Joanne replied. "You can switch to some special effects such as fade in/fade out, split screen, and superimposing titles."

"That's why it's called a 'special effects generator,' " Jenny deduced.

"The fancier models do really amazing things," Joanne continued. "This one is fairly simple: you can push a button and switch cameras, or you can use this handle you see sticking up, the fader bar, and dissolve from one picture to the other." (See Figure 4-7.)

"Does the fader bar also allow you to gradually fade from black?" Fred asked.

"Yes, you can get that effect by pressing the button that says BLACK and slowly pushing the fader bar," Joanne replied.

"This stuff is amazing," Fred said. "How does this graphics machine work?"

"That machine is called the 'character generator,' " Joanne responded. "It works something like a typewriter or a word processor. You type the message you want on the screen and press the correct button to transfer it to the recorder. You can also superimpose words on whatever picture you have going to your recorder." (See Figure 4-8.)

"That's how you superimpose titles onto shots of people," Jenny said.

"Identifying people is one of the major uses of this machine," Joanne acknowledged. "You can also type up your credits or scripture or anything else you want."

"Everything you could possibly want in a studio is right here!" Fred exclaimed.

Joanne laughed. "Not quite. We have the basics for a two-camera system, but we have a wish list for other pieces of equipment that would increase what we can do."

"What's the next thing you want?" Jenny asked.

"I want a time-base corrector, a TBC," Joanne replied.

"What's that?" asked Fred.

"Oh, a TBC does several things," Joanne said. "On a tape you have recorded, you can use it to correct the lighting of your picture or to add color."

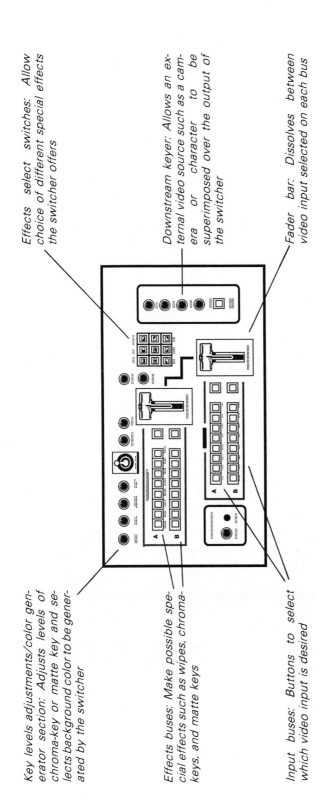

Effects select switches: Allow choice of different special effects the switcher offers

Downstream keyer: Allows an external video source such as a camera or character to be superimposed over the output of the switcher

Fader bar: Dissolves between video input selected on each bus

Key levels adjustments/color generator section: Adjusts levels of chroma-key or matte key and selects background color to be generated by the switcher

Effects buses: Make possible special effects such as wipes, chroma-keys, and matte keys

Input buses: Buttons to select which video input is desired

Figure 4-7. Special effects generator (switcher).

"The same way you would adjust the color on your television set?" Jenny was amazed.

"Right," Joanne replied, "and it's just as easy. You can also hook up the TBC to the player so that a previously recorded tape can feed right into the switcher. I'll draw this process out for you on the diagram."

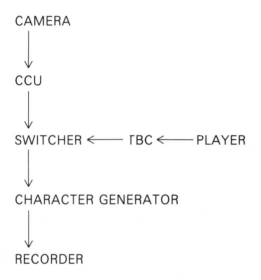

CAMERA

↓

CCU

↓

SWITCHER ⟵—— ГBC ⟵—— PLAYER

↓

CHARACTER GENERATOR

↓

RECORDER

"Is that the way you show a clip within a production?" Fred asked.

"Exactly," Joanne said. "The TBC synchronizes the clip so

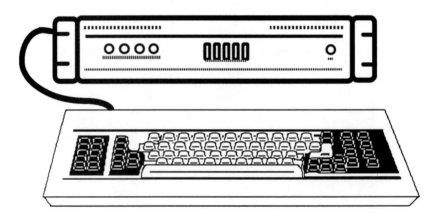

Figure 4-8. Character generator.

that it can roll in during a production. Best of all, time-base correctors are not big pieces of equipment. You can get one that's smaller than a recorder."

"Of course, without the TBC, you can still edit in the clip during post-production," Fred said.

"True," Joanne replied. "The TBC is nice but not necessary for the type of productions we do."

"Uh, you know"—Jenny carefully changed the subject— "our youth group has this play we did for our church, and—"

"Ah ha!" Joanne said. "That's why you're here. You want to produce a play in our studio."

"Well, uh—" Fred stammered.

"No problem." Joanne smiled. "You're in luck. Our church owes your pastor a favor. Last month he sent us volunteers for a community project we sponsored. I'll serve as director if you two will operate the cameras."

"That's great!" Jenny exclaimed. "But we've only worked on a one-camera production."

"Two cameras are easier," Joanne said reassuringly. "All you do is put on the camera headphones and listen to my directions. The one thing I don't want you to do is set up shots on your own. I'll be watching the monitor for each camera and telling you what to do."

"That's because you can see the whole show from the control room," Fred said. "You can coordinate it better than we can from our cameras."

"Right," Joanne replied. "I'll also adjust the iris and the white balance from the control room. All you have to do is focus and follow the action."

The play was produced with much better results than the talent show. Joanne also was happy to have two additional camera operators to add to her volunteer pool. Soon the two churches were engaged in more favor swapping, so that First Church was allowed additional usage of Parkway's studio. Fred spent many hours in the Parkway studio and eventually became a volunteer director.

CONCLUSION

The vignette in this chapter may seem fanciful but it is based more on fact than fiction. The authors regularly participate in a time-sharing arrangement for a studio serving over fifty churches. Other communities have similar arrangements. Often a few volunteers willing to learn and practice technical skills is all it takes to get started.

Some churches prefer to develop their own TV studios. Here's a step-by-step procedure for modest productions.

1. Select a room, around 25 by 25 feet, and paint the walls a medium blue or blue-green. Attach some rods to the ceiling for hanging lights and backdrops. Make sure you have at least two separate circuits with a minimum capacity of 20 amps each; more would be better.

2. If you want to plan for expansion, select two adjacent rooms, one for the studio and one for the control room. The control room can be much smaller.

3. Equipment will vary in price. Check several video stores and take bids. Get several opinions as to brands.

4. The studio can be equipped gradually over the years in add-on fashion. We recommend the following priorities:

- Purchase one camera, a recorder, an audio board, two lapel mikes, one hand-held mike with a stand, and two quartz lights to get started.
- Add the player and editing controller to complete your editing system.
- Add character generator for graphics.
- Add second camera, two camera control units, a switcher, three small monitors (one for preview), and three or four more quartz lights to complete a two-camera system. (Buying a second camera without this other equipment will not give you much of an advantage.)
- A time-base corrector is nice for synchronizing videotape machines and processing color and tint but not essential for basic productions.
- A wave-form monitor and vector scope are also nice for quality control of video but not absolutely necessary with modern cameras.
- Chroma-key and third camera are very good for superimposing backgrounds but not essential for production.

If you remember, the access studio had only a single camera and editing system. A one-camera system may be all you need for in-house productions and access programming. You also can add batteries for the camera and the recorder for outside shoots. Of course, as you continue to add equipment, the more trained volunteers you will need and the higher the maintenance costs will be. Remarkably, more and more churches are doing just that and finding it well worth the cost.

One final aspect of TV programming cannot be neglected: the talent. How you present yourself on television is an important part of production, as members of First Church realize in the next chapter.

5

Presenting Yourself on TV

Harold Jordan was sure that a thirty-minute show, starring the minister with Harold as the interviewer, would be a hit. He felt the time was now right to approach his pastor, Rev. Bob Mackintosh, with the idea of sermon interviews. Bob, however, was not as receptive as Harold would have liked.

"I'm not a media preacher," Bob objected. "And I know Carolyn would feel uncomfortable if I referred to her as 'my lovely wife' on TV."

"I'm not asking you to come on as a TV evangelist," Harold replied. "Just be yourself and let me ask you some questions about last Sunday's sermon."

"What kind of interviewer are you?" Bob asked. "Are you going to ask me tough questions and put me on the spot?"

"Of course!" Harold laughed. "I'll start off by asking where you pirate your sermon material. No, seriously, I thought we would sit down with Sharon Norris and let her guide us in what we do."

"That's not a bad idea," Bob agreed. "Sharon has had a lot of good experience on television."

Bob agreed to try one show and cancel out if it did not go well. A few days later, they met with Sharon to get some advice on how to present themselves on TV.

Interviewing on TV

"A good interviewer should ask questions that people watching the show would want to ask if they were present," Sharon began. "For example, before you get into your subject matter, Harold should ask questions about the personal life of Bob Mackintosh and let the audience get to know him. Later in the interview, if Bob uses an obscure theological term,

Harold should interrupt on behalf of the viewer and ask for a definition."

"That might cause me to forget what I'm saying," Bob objected.

"It's up to the interviewer to listen carefully and not let that happen," Sharon said. "After an interruption, Harold should say something like 'I believe you were talking about—whatever' and put you back on track. In fact, the interviewer should also notice when the interviewee is becoming too repetitious. Harold should keep the interview moving by politely injecting a comment such as 'You have been very clear on so-and-so, but I don't want us to run out of time. Could you summarize your next points so that we could get into some questions?' "

"If I'm hearing you correctly, you are suggesting a different format from a rehashing of my sermon," Bob noted.

"If you preach a twenty-minute sermon to Harold, that could be boring," Sharon answered. "I'm assuming you will want to give a three-minute synopsis and do the rest of the show with questions and answers."

"That's what I had in mind," Harold said. "Sharon, do you have any other suggestions as to how we should do this interview?"

"The most important part of the interview is in what you agree upon *before* the show," Harriet replied. "In other words, you should always do a pre-interview and outline the segments."

"You're suggesting a production plan." Harold remembered his classes with Sally Hawsley.

"That's right," Sharon replied. "You should have a clear idea of the main theme and the time frame for each subtopic or segment. For example, you might first introduce the title of the sermon and show the scripture on the screen for the first segment. Then you would have Bob summarize his main point for the second segment. After that you would agree on the amount of time you would spend in discussing each subtopic."

"We could do that just by looking over an outline of my sermon," Bob said.

"That would be a good way of identifying your topics," Sharon agreed.

"Do you have any suggestions as to how I should ask questions?" Harold wanted to know.

"A good interview starts with simple questions to clarify what the viewer is watching," Sharon replied. "Your first few questions would call for short answers. You might use the familiar journalistic technique of who, what, where, when, and why in order to give us the basic information as to what we will be seeing. The viewer will want to know who Bob is, why he is on the show, what the sermon title is, and so forth. After that, you can map out the territory by asking Bob to tell us his main point. Next you should offer open-ended questions that encourage longer answers."

"How would I do that?" Harold was intrigued.

"Asking questions with a 'how' is one example." Sharon smiled. "You might also ask questions that elicit feelings, such as 'What are your feelings about that,' or 'When that happened, what was your reaction?' You could play devil's advocate and ask 'what if' questions: for example, 'What if someone were to say that your morality is outdated?' Then you could follow up by asking 'How would you respond to that?' "

"Should I ask 'why' questions?" Harold wondered.

"Asking 'why' often will encourage a short response," Sharon replied. "You can rephrase your 'why' question and make it open-ended by asking 'What are the reasons?' When you ask 'why?' the interviewee usually will respond with only one reason. Of course, toward the end of the show when you are running out of time, a 'why' question might be good."

"Your advice as to the type of questions to ask sounds very much like what I learned in my training in counseling," Bob observed.

"Yes, but the purpose is different," Sharon responded. "A TV interviewer focuses more on the viewer and how to make the show interesting than on the emotional adjustment of the person being interviewed."

"Would the show be more interesting if I asked tough questions and put my subject on the firing line?" Harold asked.

Sharon laughed. "The problem with tough questions is that the interviewee may get stage fright and clam up. However, to make the show more interesting, you might agree on a couple of tough questions in advance of airing."

"I wouldn't object if I knew what to anticipate," Bob said.

"The dynamics of making a show interesting are more related to your enthusiasm and blend of personalities than anything else," Sharon said. "More important, the interest of the viewers increases when they perceive you as speaking personally about something important that affects their lives."

Harold and Bob worked hard in preparing their first show, which was produced at Parkway Church. Technically, the production part went smoothly; the lighting, camera work, and audio all were good. However, Harold's questions appeared strained and Bob seemed guarded and defensive in his answers. The minister of Parkway, Rev. Barry Mitchell, and some of his production crew watched the taping of the show with interest. Now and again, they whispered comments to each other, and the minister took notes. Harold wondered what they thought about the show, but they disappeared before he got a chance to ask.

Before the next taping, Harold decided to do something about how blotchy his complexion had looked under TV lighting on the first program. His wife corrected his appearance with a thin layer of neutral-base makeup and a little powder. Harold was somewhat ill at ease with makeup on, but no one said anything once they noticed how much better he looked on camera. After that, Bob started wearing makeup too. The programs steadily improved as both men became more accustomed to the cameras, and they both felt satisfied when the series of programs ended.

Two months later, Bob called Harold into the church office. He was shaking his head and laughing when Harold came in.

"We should have known what those guys were up to when they started auditing our production." Bob walked over to his VCR and inserted a videotape.

"What guys? What are you talking about?"

"Barry Mitchell and his bunch at Parkway." Bob laughed. "They watched us do our show and developed an improved version of their own. Wait till you see their production. It looks spontaneous, but I suspect it's really carefully planned."

Harold pulled up a chair and stared at Bob's TV set as the picture came on. A razzle-dazzle introduction with special effects and snappy music presented Barry Mitchell and three

Panel shows

warmly smiling panel members: a teenager, a woman in her thirties, and an older man, all with interesting faces. The title of the program was "Minister Under Fire." Mitchell did not give a synopsis of his sermon. Instead, the panel began with a good-natured attack.

"You preached a sermon on 'The Peace That Passes Understanding,'" the older man began. "But at times your *sermon* seemed to pass understanding. At least it did with me. Were you saying that the quiet times we spend in our comfortable homes have nothing to do with the peace Jesus wants us to have? I think the Lord knows that once in a while we need to get away from it all and find some peace and quiet. Were you preaching against that in your sermon?"

"Wait a minute." Barry Mitchell laughed. "You know very well that Jesus needed quiet times too. The Bible talks about Jesus withdrawing from the multitudes to find solace. I'm not against that! But the passage I'm talking about in John fourteen suggests a different sort of peace. It's the peace that prevails in the midst of a noisy storm."

"You're using preacher's language." The young person spoke up. "What difference does this peace mean to us? And what's the sense of prevailing 'in the midst of a noisy storm'? That sounds like something out of Shakespeare. How can you preach on peace, knowing the issues that face us today—racism, AIDS, social injustice, illiteracy, poverty?"

"You have just described some of the noises in the storm." Barry leaned forward. "It's up to the Christian to act as peacemaker. We can do that only if the peace of Christ is a part of our own lives."

Harold walked over to the TV set, turned it off, and slumped back down in his chair.

"I don't want to hear the rest," he muttered. "I don't care how good it is. They stole our idea."

"There's no copyright on a general idea such as interviewing ministers about their sermons." Bob smiled. "I'm glad they came up with such a great show. Barry Mitchell phoned me yesterday to say how grateful they were for our giving them the inspiration. They're getting a big response—cards, letters, everything. Their show is a hit, and ours is not. I can live with that."

"They've destroyed my peace," Harold quipped. "I suppose I'll get over it. Our program certainly looks wooden compared to theirs. I should have thought of getting an interesting panel together. But instead, my ego got in the way. I had to be the big star."

"Your heart was in the right place," Bob said consolingly. "You wanted your minister to have an interesting show."

"Now what?" Harold held up his hands in a gesture of futility. "Do we give up?"

"No, I think I learned a lot about appearing on TV in the series we completed," Bob answered. "In fact, I have an idea for a new series that I'm really excited about."

"Are you going to try to improve on what Barry Mitchell has done?" Harold asked.

"I want to do something altogether different," Bob replied.

"I would like to focus on a very important aspect of my ministry—counseling. I think I've helped more people in this way than any other."

"No argument there," Harold agreed. "You've helped many of our members through some tough times, and it's meant a lot to our church. How are you going to set up the series?"

"I'm not sure." Bob pondered the idea. "We need to talk to Sharon Norris again and let her suggest the format. I want people to catch the vision of what a good counseling program can do."

Sharon, as usual, was eager to help. She began by reviewing some of the programs produced by Harold and Bob.

"There are some little commonsense things that would have made your show look a lot better," Sharon said. "Perhaps you can incorporate them into your next series. First of all, think

Colors and movement

about the background of your set. Both of you wore blue suits against a blue background. You seemed to be deliberately trying to camouflage yourselves. Don't blend into the set. You need a contrast of colors. The other thing I noticed was the absence of body language. For the most part, although you showed some movement in your later shows, you were too stiff. Don't be afraid to move your arms occasionally or shift positions. Too much movement is distracting but so is suspended animation. On the positive side, you did not stare at the camera but talked to each other. It looked like a conversation, and that's good. You might have improved that appearance by interrupting each other now and then. Don't do it constantly, but a free-flowing conversation would be expected to have at least some break-ins. Also, you don't have to wait for the dead silence of the other before starting to talk."

"That's a lot to remember," Harold said. "We may find ourselves forgetting our subject matter if we think too much about how we look and respond."

Distracting mannerisms

"There's a very easy way to correct undesirable mannerisms," Sharon replied. "Watch every program you produce at least twice. Replays are an excellent teacher, and you will find yourselves automatically making the right changes—if you know what to look for."

"Some seminaries use videotapes to help ministers improve their sermons," Bob said.

"Most of us have mannerisms that we are unaware of until we see ourselves on TV," Sharon said. "I have a habit of adjusting my hair, but I can control it for a thirty-minute TV show."

"I thought we were supposed to relax and just be ourselves." Harold remembered what he had learned in his access training.

Sharon smiled. "That's good advice for beginners. When you are new to the business, you should concentrate on content and forget style. However, you two are now veteran TV personalities and you can afford to evaluate your presentations critically."

"I appreciate the advice on our old show," Bob said. "Now let's look at the new series I want to do. How can I format an interesting program on counseling?"

"Hmm, I should think a counseling show would be a natural for TV," Sharon said. "Do you have any talented adults in your church who could do a role play of problem situations?"

| **Role play on TV** |

"You mean like a dramatization showing a marital conflict?" Bob asked.

"Yes. Or it could be a problem situation between parent and child, or supervisor and subordinate," Sharon replied. "You might even have someone do a soliloquy about loneliness or an attempted suicide. Toward the end of the show, you might have your actors depict positive solutions. There are a number of alternatives in role play."

"How would I integrate these dramatizations into my program?" Bob was obviously excited about the idea.

"Role play is an illustration of the subject matter." Sharon thought for a moment. "You could interview a guest counselor with cuts to your role play when you want to introduce or illustrate your next point."

"How would you do that?" Bob asked.

"I would have the role play previously taped," Sharon replied. "If your studio has a time-base corrector—a TBC—you could roll in the role-play segments during your interview whenever they were appropriate. If you don't have a TBC, you'll have to edit in the role play after you finish the interview."

"We'll have to edit in the role play," Harold said, "but that's no problem. It's easy to do."

"If that's the case, then your guest should preview the role-play segments before the interview," Sharon said. "During the interview, you will need to look at the camera and pretend to watch the role play."

"I don't understand." Bob was puzzled. "Won't we be able to see the role play with the TV audience?"

"Not during the interview." Harold laughed. "Without a TBC, the role play will have to be edited in

Creating an illusion

later. To create the illusion of watching the role play, you just look into the camera and say 'Let's watch this clip.' Then pause for a few seconds so that in post-production we can make a clean edit."

"What do we do after the pause?" Bob asked.

"Well, when the program is edited, the audience will see the role play and will believe that you watched it with them," Sharon replied. "After the pause, you turn back to your guest as if both of you have seen the role play."

"Maybe it would be easier to have the actors perform at the time of the interview," Bob said.

"You'd drive your production crew crazy with that setup," Harold objected. "The role play would need different audio and lighting and probably a different set design."

"Harold's right," Sharon said. "You should script out the role-play segments so you can control the time as well as the content. That way, you'll know what to say during the interview and avoid the confusion of attempting role play and interview at the same time."

"Well, all right, we'll tape them separately. I like the idea of watching the role-play segments in advance," Bob added. "Counselors make observations as to body language and tone of voice as well as verbal content. I have some scripts on counseling situations I could use."

"You'll want to type the TV script in two columns," Sharon said. "The right-hand column is the actor's script. The left-hand column is reserved for camera instructions. I'll help you with the camera notations."

TV scripting

In the next two weeks, Bob was busy organizing his programs and lining up guests. The role play was carefully scripted and timed; the interview portion was not scripted but simply outlined, with times noted for each segment. After Sharon Norris supplied the camera notations, or cues, in the left-hand column of the script, she explained what the abbreviations meant. Bob spelled out these and other notations on his copy of the script. The day before the production, Bob thumbed through his copy with a sense of pride and accomplishment. The first part of it looked like this:

TV Script #1: Parenting

Guest: Dr. John Daniels

Camera Cues	*Script*
Note: CU = close-up of head and shoulders, MS = medium or waist shot, LS = long or established shot of all participants	The script gives the role play in sequence within the outline of the interview.
	(Title and front credits, followed by introduction of guest)
Start with CU of host, then LS, followed by CUs of each speaker as appropriate.	HOST: Today, it is my pleasure to introduce Dr. John Daniels.
	(Two minutes for introduction)
CU of host	*CUE FOR ROLE PLAY*—HOST: Let's take a look at an argument going on between a parent and child.
Fade-out Edit #1 from role-play tape	*(One-half minute for role play #1)*
Fade in to LS	PARENT: You're a slob! You never pick up after yourself. You always expect me to do it!
CU of child	CHILD: Why can't I live my own life? Why are you always telling me what to do?
CU of parent	PARENT: Just who do you think you are? I'm the parent here, and you better do what I tell you!
LS	CHILD: What are you going to do if I don't? PARENT: I'm going to tan your little hide! CHILD: You do and I'll never clean up my room again—*never!*
Fade-out	*(Parent stares in astonishment at child as scene fades)*

Camera Cues	Script
Fade-in to MS of host	HOST *(turning away from camera):* Well, now that we've seen
LS	the first act of our little drama, what comments do you have about the behavior of these two people, Dr. Daniels?
MS of guest	*(Guest makes whatever comments he would like; Host will continue to ask questions for five minutes of discussion)*
MS of host	*CUE FOR ROLE PLAY*—HOST: I wonder if the parent in our drama will use another ap-
Fade-out	proach to child discipline. Let's take a look.
Edit in role play #2	*(One-half minute for role play #2)*
Fade in, LS	PARENT: I'm going to try to reason with you. When we have a messy house, we can't find things when we need them and it's embarrassing when friends come to visit.
CU of child	CHILD: My friends won't be embarrassed. They know what my room looks like.
LS	PARENT: Well, it's embarrassing to us.
	CHILD: Not to me.
CU of parent	PARENT *(exasperated):* You can't find things when you look for them. How can you, in all this mess?
LS	CHILD: I know where my stuff is. What's the big deal?
CU of parent	PARENT *(sighs):* I give up.
Fade-out	
Fade-in to MS of host	HOST *(turning away from camera):* That conversation sounds
LS	familiar, at least it does for my family. Tell us, Dr. Daniels, is it possible to reason with a child? *(Guest and Host continue discussion for another five minutes)*

When the day for production came, the director, Joanne Blackwell, requested a minor change in the script.

"I need more time to cue the cameras for a close-up when you make your transition to the role-play segments," Joanne said. "Could you add an extra sentence that we could see in the script, such as 'Let's go back to our drama,' before you introduce it?"

"Sure, I can do that," Bob replied. "One other thing—when I wind up my five-minute interview segments, could I be given a two-minute, one-minute, and finally a thirty-second cue?"

"At the end of each five-minute segment?" Joanne asked.

"Yes. If you could give me three cues, I'd appreciate it," Bob said. "I know you hold up fingers for one and two minutes, but what sign do you make for thirty seconds?"

"The one we use is a closed fist with the palm toward you—like the old protest symbol," Joanne answered. "I'll ask the floor director to give you those cues."

Harold entered the studio and motioned Bob to come over for a private conference.

"I asked Joanne to be our director tonight because Fred is sick and couldn't make it," Harold began. "Joanne's good, but she's not used to us."

"What difference does that make?"

"Well, I don't know how to tell you this"—Harold laughed—"but you have a couple of habits I never bothered to mention because they weren't so obvious when we were working with our own people."

"What on earth are you talking about?"

"You have a bad habit of giving the camera people directions," Harold replied. "That's the director's job. Joanne will watch the monitor from the control booth and tell the camera people what to do over their headphones. Your job is to do the interview and leave the technical stuff to her."

Studio etiquette

Bob was embarrassed. "I didn't mean to be rude."

"Rudeness is not the issue," Harold explained. "No matter how polite you are, it's confusing to the production crew when they hear your suggestions from the floor and the director's instructions over their headphones."

"All right, I won't make suggestions to the camera people," Bob conceded. "But I wish they would tell me when my tie is crooked or my hair needs combing."

"They're not going to be looking for that sort of thing,"

Harold said. "The camera people are busy listening to the director and lining up their shots. Tell me something. When we appeared together on our last program, did you notice the ketchup stain on my shirt?"

"Well, not until we were in the middle of the show." Bob laughed. "I was too busy thinking about what I was going to say. I see your point. We can't depend on people involved in production to look for those details. Maybe we should recruit a special person to oversee the appearance of the set and the performers."

"That would be a good solution," Harold agreed.

The first show went very well. Counseling was at the heart of Bob's ministry, and his enthusiasm showed. The next week he received several phone calls from people who had watched the show and wanted help. Even Barry Mitchell called to congratulate him. Bob became hooked on this electronic extension of his ministry and started making a point of showing up at meetings of the media committee.

Three months later, Joanne Blackwell phoned Harold Jordan at his home with some exciting news.

"Guess what?" Joanne exclaimed. "One of your members has just donated a time-base corrector to our church in exchange for your rights to our studio."

"You mean we can use your studio anytime we want for free?" Harold was equally excited.

"Well, yes, up to six hours per week," Joanne replied.

"That's all we'll need," Harold said with satisfaction.

"This TBC model has a special effects unit that's really going to make a dramatic difference in the appearance of our shows," Joanne continued. "We can do mosaics, freeze-framing, and several other things. More important, the editing is going to look crisper and we'll have better control of our color."

"And we'll be able to roll in the role-play segments during the counseling series," Harold said. "I'll bet Mrs. Goodworthy made this possible after hearing from our minister about what such an addition would mean to his show."

"As a matter of fact, Mrs. Goodworthy *is* the donor."

"I'm not surprised," Harold said. "It just shows what can happen when your minister is meaningfully involved with your media committee. Only yesterday he was complaining that he didn't have a pair of white shoes."

"Maybe Mrs. Goodworthy will donate a pair," Joanne told him, laughing.

CONCLUSION

However good the production equipment may be, it cannot cover up a poor performance or a bad production plan. Most TV talent is made, not born. Very few of us carry an innate charisma that lights up the stage whenever the camera turns our way. Hollywood might want us to believe, for the sake of publicity, that all major motion picture actors have charisma. Some do, but if we look critically at their earlier performances, we will realize that most actors have had to work hard to develop credible portrayals. Furthermore, all of us have seen movies, loaded with famous actors, that flop because the script or the directing is poor.

What is especially sad is that intelligent church leaders who have the most to say are often the least likely to go on TV. They have seen the performances of some bubble-headed TV personalities and have come to think of these as the TV standard. They also may have had friends who braved a single TV appearance and came off looking like scared rabbits. However, as the story of Bob Mackintosh illustrates, it takes more than just one or two performances to develop TV skills.

This is not to say that acquiring the basic TV skills is difficult, nor is it true that the first performance is always a poor one. Intelligent people are not at a disadvantage on TV. In fact, they will find that they can develop TV skills quite readily. Here is a summary of the basics:

1. In your first performance, concentrate on *what* you are saying rather than *how*. Relax, be yourself, and speak in a normal voice, as you would to *one* person. Tell yourself there is no mass audience out there, just a couple of people, probably in their bathrobes, looking at their TV sets.

2. When being interviewed, talk to the interviewer and *not* to the camera. If people seem to enjoy your conversations off TV, you can safely assume that they will listen to you during a TV interview. The best interviews are free-flowing, sometimes with one person breaking in on the other. If you don't understand the interviewer's question, ask for clarification of whatever confuses you. If you don't know the answer, say so. Don't be defensive. Even with tough questions, think of the interview as a conversation, not as an examination.

3. If you are the interviewer, your most important job is in the pre-interview period before the show. You should get to know your guest and plan the program in segments, with time frames for each topic. During the program, talk to the camera

when you are introducing your guest or signing off; otherwise face your guest. At the start, ask some personal questions that will let the audience get to know the guest. Above all, concentrate on what your guest is saying so your follow-up questions will be appropriate. Nothing kills an interview faster than an interviewer who obviously has not been listening.

If your guest gets off the subject, politely bring up the topic again. If your guest becomes repetitious, politely go to the next topic. Keep your interview conversational. Don't spend your time preaching to the audience, making jokes, or flattering the guest. Your job is to bring out the informational and feeling content of what your guest has to say. You should ask questions that you think the viewer would want to ask. Remember, some guests are going to be boring no matter what you do; it won't help matters to bring out a rubber chicken.

If you are planning a panel show instead of an interview, select your panel members, if possible, to represent the age and ethnic distribution of the TV audience. Choose people who are good conversationalists with animated, interesting faces. Most important, they should be credible, with personal knowledge of the topic.

If you are the production manager or director of a panel show, make sure that the mike check is done with one mike at a time, with the other mikes turned down. When people are sitting close together, they may "bleed" over into the other mikes and cause a false needle reading. The result of such an improper mike check is a hollow sound.

4. As you become a veteran TV performer, critically review your tapes for mannerisms and habitual behavior that distract from your appearance. Don't overcorrect your habits by becoming too stiff; some motion is desirable.

The media committee, chaired by Harriet Wingate, has successfully worked its way into TV production. As important as television is, a multimedia approach is needed to make the church fully effective within the congregation and the community. The attention of the committee can now turn to the advantages and special requirements of audio production. This knowledge is also essential if they are to go from passable to good audio in their TV production.

6

Audio Production: Developing a Cassette Ministry

Harriet Wingate discovered an expert in audio production on her media committee. This was none other than Fred Wells, who had already become their volunteer technical director for TV productions. Although Fred was only a senior in high school, he had three years of audio experience with a teenage vocal group. He also had a part-time job as a DJ for a local radio station. Harriet felt lucky that Fred continued to fit the media committee into his busy schedule.

Fred brought an array of equipment to the first meeting on audio production.

"This stuff is a lot easier than producing TV shows," he began. "But I paid more money than I should have for some of this equipment. You can profit from my mistakes."

"Ah, the voice of experience!" Harold laughed.

"The first thing I would advise is to avoid using those dinky little mono cassette recorders that we have in our Sunday school classrooms," Fred said.

Jane frowned. "Are you saying we have to get rid of our cassette recorders?"

"No, don't do that," Fred replied. "They're fine for small classrooms. But if you want to record the worship service, you should use a good stereo cassette recorder."

"How much money are we talking about?" Mark asked.

Selecting equipment

"Watch the ads. You can get a fairly good one on sale for not much more than the classroom type," Fred said. "The better decks give you a better quality sound. You also get such useful features as noise reduction and the capacity for high-quality tapes."

"I don't like the way my voice sounds on a cassette recorder," Martha said.

"The sound gets better with open-reel recordings and microphones," Fred responded. "The higher the speed of the tape, the better the audio. For example, a cassette records at one and seven-eighths inches per second. At my radio station, our open reel records at seven and a half inches per second on the slow speed and fifteen inches per second on the high speed."

"Maybe we should get an open-reel recorder," Mark said.

"Well, a good stereo cassette recorder is adequate for voices," Fred replied. "A cassette is much easier to use than an open reel and should work fine for our purposes."

"Exactly what are our purposes?" Harold wanted to know.

"Our congregational care committee has asked us to develop an audiocassette ministry for homebound members and for our prison ministry," Harriet explained. "Apparently, the volunteers who regularly make these visits are willing and eager to deliver the cassettes. Their committee keeps track of these visits, and when a visit is missed the cassette can be mailed."

"If the minister preaches an especially good sermon, members who are absent that day might benefit from our audiocassette ministry too," Martha pointed out. "We should keep copies in our church library."

"What about audio for the choir?" Jane asked. "Would a cassette work for that?"

"Yes, if we use the right mikes," Fred answered. "I would recommend using two low-impedance unidirectional mikes for the choir."

"What does that do?" Mark asked.

"A low-impedance mike allows you to use a longer cord and position your mikes in front of the person or group you are recording," Fred replied. "If the mike is too far away, you get a bottom-of-the-barrel sound. With a high-impedance mike, anything over a twenty-foot cord won't give you good audio."

"Explain what you mean by unidirectional," Harriet requested.

"A unidirectional mike is one that picks up sound mostly in front of the microphone. Of course, you have to select one that is either low-impedance or high-impedance," Fred said. "I might add that a transformer is needed to make a low-impedance mike work with most recorders."

"How much is a transformer going to cost us?" Jane inquired.

"You can get one for the price of a good screwdriver." Fred reached into his equipment bag. "Here's what they look like.

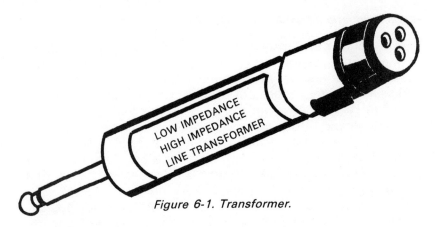

Figure 6-1. Transformer.

You hook up the transformer between the mike cord and the recorder." (See Figure 6-1.)

"What about hooking up the recorder to the amplifier of the PA system?" Harold asked.

Fred thought for a moment. "There are two problems with that. First of all, the only outputs to some amplifiers are the main ones designed for the *speaker* system. If you hook up the *recorder* to the main amp, you'll probably overload your recorder and burn it out. Some amplifiers do carry an output with a low-voltage 'pre-amp' that allows you to hook up the recorder safely. But even with that, you run into a second problem—the mike is too far away from the choir and only the preacher gets a good recording."

"How do you hook up mikes for the choir and the preacher on the same recorder?" Mark wondered.

"You use a mixer." Fred picked up a piece of equipment from the table. "Like this one." (See Figure 6-2.)

"Does this mixer work the same way as the one in the TV studio?" Jane asked.

"Right," Fred said. "You hook up the mixer to the recorder and the mikes to the mixer. Then you set the knobs and levers to get the sound level you want."

"Where do you put the transformer?" Mark asked.

"If you buy a mixer like this one with low-impedance inputs, you don't need it," Fred replied.

"A mixer can cost anywhere from two hundred dollars up," Harold said.

"If you buy a mixer with hookups for just four mikes," Fred told him, "you can keep the cost down and it will work fine."

"So we need a stereo cassette recorder, four mikes, a mixer, and some blank tapes," Harriet summarized.

"The one other item I would like to see us buy is a high-speed duplicator," Fred said. "You can get one that duplicates sixteen tapes in one hour for about the price of a TV set."

"Whoa." It was Harold again. "How much money are we going to spend on this project? Do we really need a duplicator?"

"If you shop around, the total package—mikes, duplicator, and everything—would cost about the same as a good home stereo system," Fred replied. "What good does it do to have a cassette ministry if it takes all day to copy tapes?"

"We can't afford it," Mark said flatly.

"I'll tell you what," Fred suggested. "I'm convinced the church really needs an audiocassette ministry. If you'll buy the duplicator and tapes, I'll offer my equipment and services free for the rest of the year. I will also organize a fund drive among the young people to replace my stuff. If I don't succeed, you can keep whatever equipment I fail to replace."

"Hmm." Harriet thought for a moment. "Fred is making us a very generous offer. Maybe I can get my adult Sunday school class to match what the young people raise."

The media committee knew Fred would try hard to keep his promise. They bought the duplicator, and Fred organized a

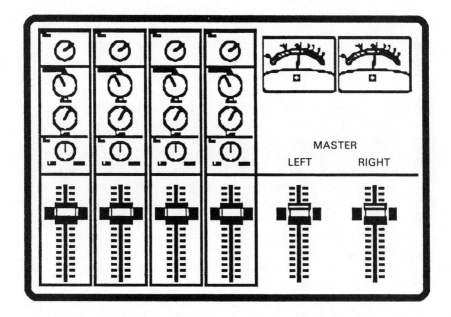

Figure 6-2. Audio mixer.

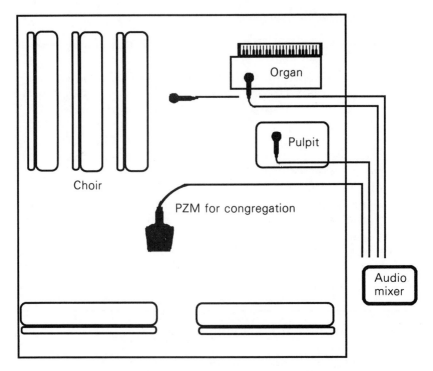

Figure 6-3. Configuration of audio equipment.

team of three young people to work with him. Only one person at a time was needed to make the recordings, but Fred wanted to be sure he had enough backups. He also reasoned that by enlisting his friends to install the equipment, they would become more interested in running it.

When Fred met with his cohorts to set things up, he produced a diagram showing the configuration for the mikes.

"Here's what I want." Fred pointed to his drawing. "We have four mikes; you can see their positions." (See Figure 6-3.)

"Let's see." Jenny Barnes examined the diagram. "You've got a mixer with four mikes coming out from it. I suppose you'll clamp the mike for the pulpit under the PA mike."

"Right," Fred said. "We don't have a pre-amp output from the amplifier, so we can't run a line out from the amplifier and use the pulpit mike. We'll have to use a second mike on the pulpit for the recorder."

"What's this mike for the congregation?" asked Charlie Hunt, one of Fred's other recruits.

"Well, we only have one lectern, so that leaves us an extra mike," Fred replied. "It occurred to me, after I talked with the media committee, that our homebound members might enjoy hearing the congregational singing and scripture responses as well as the sermon."

"Are you going to use an omnidirectional mike?" Jenny asked.

"I could," Fred said, "but it would pick up sounds all over the place, including reflected sounds bouncing off the walls."

"Then you'll use a unidirectional mike."

"Nope." Fred laughed. "That also would pick up reflected sounds."

Using the right mike

"What's left?" asked Bill Johnson, the third recruit.

"Look in my equipment bag and see if you can guess," Fred said.

"I wish you'd stop treating us like children," Jenny said with irritation as she looked through the equipment bag. "Some of these mikes are labeled omnidirectional and others aren't labeled at all. Why don't you stop fooling around and show us which one you mean?"

"All right." Fred reached into his bag and produced a strange-looking device. "I'm going to use this one. It's called a pressure-zone mike—a PZM, for short." (See Figure 6-4.)

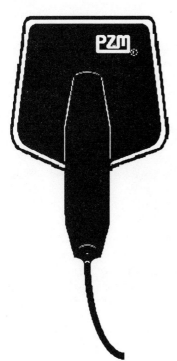

Figure 6-4. PZM microphone.
(PZM is a trademark of Crown U.S.A.)

"That doesn't even look like a mike," Charlie said. "How do you use it?"

"You have to put it against a flat surface. Probably we'll attach it to a wall," Fred replied. "The advantage of a PZM is that it won't pick up reflected sounds and it doesn't give way to a proximity effect."

"Oh, that's just great," Bill said with a mock grin. "How about telling us what that means?"

"The proximity effect has to do with the fact that, with most mikes, the closer you get, the greater the bass," Fred explained. "The PZM tends to avoid that effect; it reduces the boominess and cuts down on extraneous sounds. You wouldn't want to use it for the preacher, but it's a good choice for the congregation."

"Your equipment bag raises some questions," Jenny observed. "How can you tell which mikes are which?"

"You can tell which mikes are low-impedance by the three-prong pins on the connectors." Fred reached for the mikes in his bag. "High-impedance mikes use a telephone jack like this one." (See Figure 6-5.)

"How do you know when a mike is unidirectional or omnidirectional?" Jenny persisted.

"You can't always tell that," Fred acknowledged. "Most mikes look alike. When you buy one, it's a good idea to label it."

"OK," Jenny said. "Do we use an omnidirectional mike for the choir?"

"I think we'll go with unidirectional," Fred replied. "The sound will be better if it's focused in one direction. We'll need one for the choir and one for the organ."

"So we're using a PZM for the congregation and unidirectional mikes for the pulpit, the choir, and the organ," Charlie summarized.

"Yes and all these mikes will be low-impedance," Fred added.

"Why not go with shorter cords and high-impedance?" Bill inquired.

"If you're too close to the source of the sound, it's difficult to figure out the audio level," Fred responded. "We need low-impedance in order to use longer cords and set up our mixer and recorder in the hallway closet. That way we can open the closet door on Sunday and have one of you sitting in a chair next to it as the audio operator."

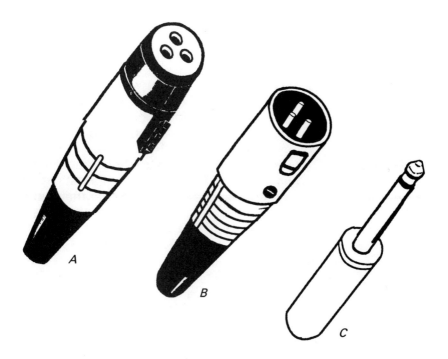

Figure 6-5. Low- and high-impedance connectors.
A 3-prong female connector
B 3-prong male connector
C ¼-inch phone jack

"I'm curious about something," Charlie announced. "When do you use an omnidirectional mike?"

"Usually when you want to pick up the sounds around you," Fred answered, "such as an audience or street interview with only one mike. We won't need one for what we're doing here."

"I guess the next step is to run the cable cords to the places we want them." Jenny was anxious to get started. "We'll need a stapler to tack them along the baseboards so they won't be noticed."

Audio cables

"No, we don't want to use a stapler," Fred said. "The sheathing of audio cables holds a brittle wire that staples could break. In fact, that's why I wrap my cables in large circles so there are no sharp bends. Even if the sheathing remains unbroken, you still could break the wire inside. I have some little U-shaped nails and a hammer for the baseboards, but go easy on the hammer."

"What if our church already had a public-address system with a mixer?" Bill wondered. "Could we run a line feed from the mixer to the recorder and control both systems with the same mixer?"

"Yes, we could," Fred replied, "but you would be trying to do two different things with one mixer. You would either get a good recording with a mediocre PA or vice versa. For example, you might turn up the choir to get a good recording level and blast out the congregation on the PA."

The three recruits followed Fred's instructions and gently tacked the audio cables from the hallway to their destination points in the sanctuary. Afterward, they looked over their work to make sure that both cables and mikes were unobtrusive.

"Oh, no!" Jenny said. "Do you see what we've done?"

Fred was puzzled. "It looks good to me."

"Yes, but we ran one of our cables next to an AC power cord coming out from the wall socket," Jenny replied.

Fred looked again. "You're so right!"

"What's wrong with running a cable next to an AC cord?" Charlie asked.

"It'll pick up the AC current, and our recording will have a hum," Jenny answered. "We'll have to reroute one or the other. It's all right if they run exactly perpendicular but not parallel or at an angle. The best way is to be sure the two are separated. We learned that in our TV classes."

After some refiguring, the cables were properly routed and connections were made from the mixer to the recorder. Two of the teenagers tested the mikes by singing and talking in the sanctuary while the other two made test recordings from the hallway.

"Won't the sound be different when the sanctuary is filled with people?" Bill asked.

"That's a problem for a PA system, not for our recording system," Fred replied. "We're not concerned with how the sound travels out into the sanctuary. We just want to get the audio from our mikes to the recorder. Let's gather around the mixer and I'll show you what needs to be done on Sundays."

Operating the audio mixer

"All we do is put on the headphone and turn the knobs and adjust the levers for the audio, right?" Charlie asked.

"Well, almost." Fred smiled. "You should also turn down the mikes of the choir when the preacher is speaking and vice versa. The same thing is true with the mikes to the congregation and the organ. However, if the preacher tells a joke, you might turn up the mike to the congregation to get their reaction."

"So when the choir is singing, we turn off the mikes to the congregation and the pulpit," Charlie said.

"Right. And you should adjust the mike to the organ so that it doesn't drown out the choir. Also, check on the position of the mike for the choir. If it gets too close to one person, that voice will be heard above all the others."

"Why do we need to use the headphone?" Charlie asked. "Why not simply judge what's happening by the needles on the volume unit of the mixer?"

"You need to do both," Fred replied. "The headphone tells you when you are getting imbalances or unnecessary sounds and when your bass and treble need to be adjusted. You should watch the needle so that it normally goes up to the red but not in it. Don't keep turning the volume up and down. Make only minor adjustments, once you've set the level."

"Where's the adjustment for the bass and treble?" Bill asked.

"This particular mixer has an equalizer for that," Fred said. "Do you see the letters 'EQ' next to these two knobs? (See Figure 6-6.) EQ is short for equalizer. These are the knobs to adjust for the bass and treble."

"I'm going to give it lots of bass," Charlie said.

"That sort of adjustment is fine for fooling around on your stereo at home," Fred told him, "but not for a good audio production. You don't want too much of one over the other.

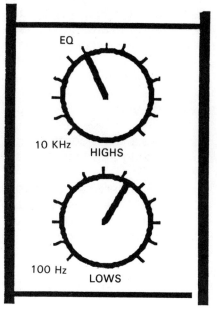

Figure 6-6.
Highlight of EQ on mixer.

Here again, make only minor adjustments with the EQ. If you hear a tinny sound, turn down the treble just a notch or turn up the bass. If the audio sounds too mellow, turn up the treble a little."

"Which sound is likely to predominate?" Bill asked.

"The bass sends out a much longer sound wave than the treble," Fred said. "In a large room, some of the treble tones are lost, so you will probably need to turn up the treble to compensate."

"Do all mixers have equalizers?" Jenny asked.

"No, they don't, but I think we need one for our purposes."

"Will our recordings work for radio?" Charlie asked.

"Probably, with the high-quality tapes we'll be using," Fred replied. "Most radio stations will dub the cassette onto an open reel. It's a convenient procedure but not as good as direct open-reel recording."

"When we make duplications of these tapes for the congregation, should the copies also be high quality?" Jenny was thinking about the expense.

Duplicating and editing

"No, the copies for the congregation can be of a lesser quality," Fred answered. "The original needs to be top-notch, just as you would want a clearly typed letter as the original for producing photocopies. The copy loses a little bit of clarity from the original. A copy of a copy is even worse. The same thing is true of both audio and video recordings. When you get down to the fourth and fifth generations (a copy of a copy of a copy, and so on), you begin to have 'dropouts'—a loss of signal or control track. That can be a problem in editing when you work from a copy instead of the original raw footage."

"When you edit an audiocassette, do you need any special equipment?" asked Jenny.

"Not really," Fred replied. "It's not like a video control track. All you have to do is stop your recording and start it again when you are ready for your next edit."

"So if we wanted to edit the worship service down to a half-hour production for radio, we would start and stop the recording from one cassette to another," Jenny concluded.

"Right. And for radio I would use high-quality tapes and do my editing with two good recorders."

"Wouldn't you need a narrator to fill in the gaps?" Bill asked.

"Sure." Fred thought for a moment. "Sometime after the

service, we can record the narrator's part and edit it in wher-
ever we want on the master."

"What do you mean by master?" Charlie asked.

"It's the copy on which we compile our final edits," Fred
answered.

"Shouldn't we make another master for the congregation?"
Bill wondered. "Some parts of the service, such as the offer-
tory, might not make for good listening."

"The media committee can decide on that one," Fred replied. "They may want the same master for the congregation
as the radio station."

At the next meeting of the media committee, the members
listened to various parts of the recorded worship service. Then
they began to make suggestions for the final edited version.

"Maybe we should look toward radio and use the same
version for the congregation," Mark said.

"What parts should we include?" Harriet asked.

"I like the congregational singing," Martha said.

"If we included all three hymns, that would make it too
long," Jane objected.

"Why not include just two hymns with two verses of each?"
Harold suggested.

"That's not a bad idea for the introduction and the ending,"
Mark agreed. "The narrator could make a short opening statement—something like 'You are listening to First Church at
worship with the Reverend Bob Mackintosh'—and then edit in
the hymn as the intro."

"After that, we'd go right into the scripture reading, the
anthem, and the sermon," Harold added.

"And then we could conclude with two verses of the last
hymn and a sign-off by the narrator," Jane said.

"I think the narrator should give the location of our church
and the time of the worship service," Martha said.

"All right." Harriet paused for a moment. "We're in agreement as to what should be included. What happens if we go
under or over thirty minutes? How do we build in some flexibility?"

"If we run short, we can always add some more verses of the
hymns and include a longer narration at the end," Harold said.

"What happens if we run long? What do we cut?" Harriet
asked.

"Well, we don't want to cut the choir," Martha stated.

"Why not cut the last hymn and use the anthem as the ending?" Mark suggested.

"Maybe Bob would let us edit out part of his sermon," Harold said.

"Never!" Harriet laughed. "Our flexibility has to be with the hymns and the anthem. If it's really tight, we may have to edit out both hymns. And if that doesn't do it, we can think about cutting part of the anthem or the scripture. Bob repeats a lot of his scripture verses within the sermon, anyway."

"I like the idea of a half-hour tape," Jane said. "Most people are not going to listen passively for a full hour; it's not the same as actively participating at church."

"Even so, there might be some homebound person who would want to hear the full service," Mark noted.

"Let's try the shorter version first," Harold said. "If we get any complaints, we can always go back to the drawing board."

"The next thing we need to do is find out if we can afford to put our service on radio," Harriet said.

"We'll also want to look at audience surveys," Jane added. "Since most radio stations are included in these surveys, we can select a station that appeals to the type of audience who would be most likely to listen to our worship service."

The recording of the worship service was edited into half-hour productions, and copies were made for the congregation. No one complained about the shorter version, and it became a popular checkout item at the church library.

An investigation of radio costs revealed that one of the least expensive times was from 6:30 to 7 A.M. on Sundays. Fred assured the committee that this time was a good one for religious-oriented listeners. Since other times were either undesirable or prohibitively expensive, the committee voted to give the 6:30 A.M. slot a try for six months. They were surprised by the number of homebound persons from First Church who tuned in. Apparently, some of the older members preferred listening to the radio to using a cassette recorder.

CONCLUSION

First Church discovered a way to make the same production serve two purposes. The primary purpose of their audiocassette ministry was to meet the needs of homebound persons and others. By using the proper equipment to make a good production, they were also able to offer their worship service to the community through radio. Even if this use of radio were to prove ineffective, the audiocassette ministry would still provide a valuable service to members of the congregation.

The principles of production are basically the same for both audio- and videocassette recording. Getting the mike close to the speaker, using several mikes in a large room, and turning down mikes that aren't being used will always make a difference. Common sense plays a part—for example, oiling squeaky doors and ceiling fans and keeping mikes away from air-conditioner vents. It also is important to learn the purposes of different types of mikes, such as omnidirectional and unidirectional. Very few audio productions, except with recordings of a single speaker, can be attempted successfully without a mixer.

Probably the most logical place for church audio productions is the worship service. It is relatively simple and inexpensive and offers a continual service, Sunday after Sunday—especially to homebound persons who have few opportunities to share in the life of the church.

Now that the media committee has considered the forms of electronic production, to complete the picture they need to look at print production. Probably the most common printed communication is the newsletter sent from the church to congregation.

7

Print Production: Newsletters, Computers, and Networking

For the past thirty years, George Wycliff had faithfully written, edited, and produced the First Church newsletter. Only a small portion of the congregation, mostly those who were George's lifelong friends, read past the first page. George believed in conserving space by using small print and filling the newsletter with as many words as possible. Indeed, his older friends had to use a magnifying glass to get through the publication.

The day came when George retired and the media committee was asked to take over the newsletter. Although some of the committee members were not excited about this project, Harriet was delighted. At one time, she had edited a small-town newspaper and knew the importance of print media.

Harriet convinced the committee to allow her to form a small subcommittee to reorganize the newsletter. To her surprise, Bill Henson, who rarely spoke up at meetings, was eager to help. Bill was an accountant who did most of his work with a computer. Martha Randels, a journalism major in college, also volunteered to serve on the subcommittee. Harriet invited Bill and Martha to her house for their first meeting.

Designing a newsletter

"I want to keep this subcommittee small," Harriet began. "We need to work closely together in redesigning what George did. I have several newsletters from other churches to start our thinking."

"Hmm." Martha looked over the sample newsletters. "One of these is really fancy—obviously done by photo-offset."

"That's way beyond our budget," Bill noted.

"I think the church that puts out this newsletter has a member who owns a printshop," Harriet said. "Perhaps they get a discount. But besides cost, the disadvantage of using a professional printer is lead time. The news can be old before it gets printed."

"Maybe that's why they only have a few articles and a monthly calendar of events," Bill said.

"Here's another newsletter that does just the opposite." Martha picked up a sample. "It's loaded with pieces on every subject imaginable."

"Look at that one closely." Harriet moved her chair next to Martha's. "It has some advantages and disadvantages. The worst part is that there's very little white space. The margins are narrow and it's difficult to read because it's all one big body of print with no columns. However, it has a number of contributing writers, which makes it interesting."

"Some of these articles are poorly written," Martha observed. "They need a good editor."

"I still would prefer this one to ours," Bill said. "All we have is a long-drawn-out epistle of one man's view of the church and a meditation by the minister."

"Getting that many writers to submit articles within the newsletter deadline must be a horrendous job," Martha commented.

"Now you've hit the nail on the head," Harriet said. "As a matter of fact, the coordinator of this newsletter is giving up the job for that very reason. It takes forty to fifty phone calls to get everybody's submissions for one issue. After that, there's no time left for editing. The participation is wonderful but the cost in time is terrible, and so is the quality of the writing."

"What they need is a compromise with just three or four good writers on the staff of the paper," Martha concluded.

"Couldn't people still make submissions?" Bill asked.

Harriet laughed. "You would have to accept every article, no matter how poor. People can be very sensitive about rejected or heavily edited articles. You could lose members."

"Well, maybe some people occasionally could be invited to do feature articles," Bill said.

"That might work," Harriet conceded. "People do need to feel that it's *their* newsletter and not just the views of one or two members."

"Using a variety of writers is not the only way to create that feeling," Martha suggested. "A variety of subject matter, mentioning congregational members by name, can develop an even better sense of participation."

"Yes, that's true," Harriet said. "People like to see their names in print, especially in association with a project or program they like. One of the things we need to do is outline our church's program and make sure our coverage includes all parts of it."

Bill picked up another newsletter from Harriet's samples.

"Now, here's a winner." Bill smiled. "It's visually appealing, with lots of graphics and pictures. And the print is attractive and large enough for anyone to read."

"I thought you'd like this one," Harriet said. "It's done with a computer and has lots of pizzazz."

"It's much too cute," Martha objected. "Look at the headings of these articles: 'Minister Fires Up Board,' 'Youth Group Conquers Paint Project,' 'Church School Explodes with New Classes'!"

Newsletter headings

"That's better than the dull titles in our newsletter," Bill rejoined, "such as 'Minister Meets with Board Members' and 'Youth Group Paints Rooms.' At least their newsletter catches your attention."

"You can catch attention without overexaggerating," Harriet said. "I like the one for the youth group, but they might have done better with 'Minister Challenges Board Members' and 'Exciting New Classes Offered.' "

"The rules in journalism are simple," Martha said. "Use short descriptive titles and active verbs that appeal to the senses, and avoid nondescript verbs and forms of 'to be.' An interesting, colorful title is desirable, but a hyperbole overloads it. The other thing I don't like in this newsletter is the way they use some of their pictures. They have no relationship to the content of the articles. Also, the print is a little *too* large—more like something you would see in a first-grade primer."

"Those are good points," Harriet said. "Style and substance ought to go together. Maybe the producers of this newsletter are just having fun with a new computer."

"Now that's what we need!" Bill exclaimed. "The right computer would make all the difference."

"Our church officers are thinking about getting a computer," Harriet said. "In fact, Jane Hardgrove is chairperson of the planning committee. Why don't you talk to her?"

"I'll do that," Bill replied. "Some computers are much better adapted for getting out newsletters than others."

"What equipment does the church have now?" Martha asked.

"We have a choice between the mimeograph and the copier," Harriet answered. "George used the mimeograph with preprinted masthead paper."

Newsletter equipment

"You mean the logo and newsletter caption were done professionally by a printer?" Bill asked.

"That's right," Harriet replied. "He allowed room for the text underneath the masthead on the mimeograph stencil."

"Our old mimeograph doesn't give a very sharp print," Martha said.

"Most mimeograph machines have that problem," Harriet noted. "The church copier is a little more expensive to use, but it does a better job."

"If we used the copier, we could buy rubdown letter sheets for headlines," Martha said. "It takes a little time to rub on the letters, but the headings would look really good."

Bill laughed. "A computer would do an even better job in a hundredth of the time."

"Well, we have to make do with what we've got," Harriet responded.

"I've got a better idea," Bill said. "I'll do the titles on the computer in my office and we'll paste them on. I'd do the whole newsletter, but I don't think my boss would let me get away with it."

"Does our church have a clip service for newsletter graphic and picture inserts?" Martha asked.

"Yes. George rarely used them, but we have some in our file," Harriet replied. "We can cut them out and paste them in."

"Won't the copier show the lines of the cutout?" Bill asked.

"If necessary, we can use liquid paper on the edges," Harriet said. "That will keep the copier from printing the outline of the clip or anything else we paste in."

Style and content

"Do we have a lighted display table with a transparent grid to center our work?" Martha inquired.

"George built a homemade version with a glass top and a light underneath," Harriet replied. "He also drew some lines on a transparent paper to act as a grid. We have the basic equipment. Let's talk about style and content."

"I assume we'll use a journalistic style," Martha said.

"Well, not a factual news-reporting style," Harriet said. "A conversational style, such as you would use in a feature story about a friend, might go over better in a church newsletter. Of course, we'll want to get in the five W's: who, what, where, when, and why. But a clinical reporting of the facts might seem too stilted."

"I'm not sure I understand what you mean." Martha was puzzled.

"Let me think of an example." Harriet paused for a moment. "Suppose you were writing a story about the youth group retreat. The facts are *Who:* the youth group; *What:* the retreat; *Where:* Okifanoche, the church regional campgrounds; *When:* the first two weeks of June; and *Why:* a variety of reasons, including fun, fellowship, and study. The outcome of this retreat was that even though it rained every day, they still had a good time and came home inspired. As a journalist, how would you write up those facts?"

"Hmm." Martha took up the challenge. "I would title the article 'Wet but Inspired.' Then I would say:

"Rain failed to dampen the spirits of the First Church youth group during the recent retreat at Camp Okifanoche.

"Both weeks of the June retreat were spent inside, as speakers and inspirational leaders addressed the group. Despite the fickle weather, First Church Youth Director June Taylor said that the speakers were the best in her memory.

" 'As the rain poured off the roof, the young people actively participated in the discussions,' Taylor said. 'Perhaps the rain was a blessing in disguise.' "

"That's pretty good," Harriet acknowledged. "But how about choosing a title that better identifies the participants and partly tells the story, such as 'Camp Deluge Fails to Dampen Youthful Spirits'? Then you could use the comments of young people to tell the story, like this:

" 'Wow! Boy, what a great retreat!' Remarks like this were typical when First Church's young people arrived back home from their June retreat at Camp Okifanoche.

" 'It rained the whole time but that didn't stop us. The food, fun, speakers—everything was terrific. I really hated to leave,' said Johnny Smith, the president of the youth group.

"Parents could hardly believe their ears as the young folks recounted one adventure after another. Rev. Bob Mackintosh remarked, 'If it was that good, I'm going next time!' Maybe we should all take advantage of our church camp conferences."

Bill laughed. "I'm ready to go to Camp Okifanoche myself after that rendition."

"So what you're suggesting is a journalism style with a down-home personalized touch," Martha concluded.

"Well, some articles would be less folksy than others, depending on the subject matter," Harriet replied. "My point is that we are not writing to a group of unknown subscribers but to friends and family. A factual news account in that setting would seem inappropriate."

"I'll go along with that," Martha said. "But the rules of journalism would still apply."

"Sure, we'll use short sentences, short paragraphs, and clear descriptions," Harriet agreed. "The primary goal of the newsletter is to get information out. The basic procedure is the same as for a newspaper. We should sum up the story in the first paragraph, followed by the next important fact in the second paragraph, and so forth. That way, if we must cut down the length, we can cut the last paragraph and not lose important details."

"I know that certain subject areas such as worship, the church school, the choir, and meetings of various kinds will be included in most of our newsletter issues," Bill said. "But what about human-interest stories focusing on a single personality or an anecdote coming from one of our members? Should those sorts of things be included?"

"By all means," Harriet replied. "Human-interest stories give vitality to a newsletter. One of the newsletters in my sample batch has a CHURCHMOUSE corner reserved for just such stories. Of course, humorous items should be favorable and not embarrassing. You can bet everyone will read them. When we write up an anecdote, we should include enough details so that readers outside the church can appreciate it too."

"Will our newsletter go to outsiders?" Bill asked.

"I hope so," Harriet responded. "The newsletter is a good vehicle to encourage outside interest in us."

"I've seen other newsletters that talk about past events," Martha said. "Sometimes it'll be a memory of an event that occurred fifteen or twenty years ago during the same month of the newsletter issue."

"Older people would love that." Harriet smiled. "One of the good things George Wycliff did was to keep a newsletter file. We can dig out those old memories and have a corner entitled THE WAY WE WERE or PAST RECOLLECTIONS."

"I suppose we should include an article on denominational news," Bill said.

Martha agreed. "Especially if it's news that directly affects our church."

"What about cartoons? Jane Hardgrove is very talented in that area," Bill noted.

"Cartoons are great. Obviously, we're not going to run short of ideas," Harriet said. "I'm sure the media committee will have some thoughts too. As an overall objective, we should make certain that the stories we run are newsworthy."

"How do you determine newsworthiness?" Bill wondered.

"A good story should make some sort of difference," Harriet replied. "It should provide a fresh insight, inspiration, needed information, or at least something new mixed with the old that causes us to think and become more aware. If a story has no potential for influencing, informing, or entertaining us in some beneficial way, we shouldn't run it."

"Should you repeat a story more than once?" Martha asked.

"Yes, if it's a story about an important event," Harriet replied. "For example, Youth Sunday might be announced in one issue with a discussion of the young people's plans for the worship service. Afterward we can tell what happened, perhaps with pictures, in the next issue."

"We could also do a feature story on the main speaker," Bill added.

"Probably we wouldn't treat a follow-up article as the lead story," Harriet noted. "Normally, the older the story, the farther down in the newsletter it should appear."

The subcommittee reported back to the media committee, and a brainstorming session ensued. The following list was produced to identify potential areas for newsletter articles:

- Worship service (new sermon series, special music, or guest speaker
- Church school (new classes, curriculum changes, or feature story on a teacher)
- Regular meetings (special events with youth and adults)
- Choral performances (cantatas, concerts)
- Fellowship dinners (featured speakers, entertainment)
- Camps and conferences
- Interfaith meetings
- Community outreach programs
- Denominational events
- Promos (stewardship, volunteer enlistment)
- Human interest stories

The improvements in the First Church newsletter brought a flood of requests from members asking that their friends' names be added to the address files. Fortunately, the church had already applied at the post office for bulk-rate postal privileges, so the increased mailing expense was not significant. However, adding new addresses to the old addressograph machine proved messy and burdensome. Also, each issue of the newsletter took several hours to lay out. Finally, the church officers gave approval to Jane Hardgrove's committee to purchase a new computer. Bill Henson met with Jane to share his experience with computers.

"The most expensive computer is not necessarily the one we want," Bill began. "We want a user-friendly model with enough storage and program features to take care of our needs."

Choosing a computer

"I know of other churches who thought they had enough storage space and ran out," Jane said. "Furthermore, those so-called user-friendly models can take several months to get used to."

"Did those churches stop using their computers?" Bill smiled, knowing the answer.

"Of course not," Jane said. "You and I both know that computers soon become indispensable. However, I don't want to buy so inexpensive a computer that it runs out of space and won't give us what we need."

"Well, in general, the newer models have much more space and many more features than the old ones," Bill said. "Also, the market is larger now. We can check with owners and see how they like their particular models."

"Since you've had some experience, let's start with *you*," Jane said. "I know that a computer program comes prerecorded on a tape or disk. What sort of programs do we need for our computer?"

"In my opinion," Bill replied, "we need a word-processing program for writing letters, a data-base program for addresses, a finance program for the church budget, a graphics program for illustrations and charts, and a layout or page-making program for the newsletter and bulletin. The computer we get should do a good job in all those areas. It would also be nice to get a scanner so that the computer can copy photographs."

"I'm not at all clear on any of this!" Jane confessed.

"Don't worry." Bill laughed. "Every computer salesperson we visit will delight in demonstrating those programs, as well as others."

Jane's committee, with Bill's help, spent six weeks in comparing computers, checking with owners, reading consumer reports, and finally making a decision. The computer they bought, not surprisingly, was the same model as Bill's. The church secretary, who viewed the new machine with awe and fear, kept Bill's phone number taped to the screen.

After a few months, the advantages of the computer were obvious to anyone who read the newsletter. One day, Harold started questioning Bill Henson about the changes in the newsletter. Together, they studied the front page of an issue of the First Church newsletter produced by the computer. (See Figure 7-1.)

"I'm trying to figure out why this newsletter is such a big improvement over the old one," Harold said. "Does our new computer get the credit?"

"Well, the newsletter was a success before we got the computer," Bill said. "Harriet and Martha are responsible for that; they determined the style of writing, the type of articles, and the layout. For example, they use a two-column layout with short paragraphs and sentences. That means an easy-to-read newsletter with lots of white space."

"Why is white space so important?" Harold asked.

"White space—any area without print on it—divides the text into small chunks and gives the newsletter its reading appeal. Pictures help in the same way."

"What difference does the computer make?" Harold studied the newsletter.

"The computer dresses up the newsletter so that people are attracted to it even before they read it," Bill said proudly.

"Give me some examples," Harold persisted.

Computerized newsletters

"For one thing, look at the density and clarity of print," Bill pointed out.

"It looks almost as good as offset," Harold commented.

"That's because we print out the original on a laser printer," Bill said.

"The church can't afford a laser printer," Harold responded.

"That's right, and we don't need one that often," Bill agreed. "But we found a downtown copy shop with a computer like ours *and* a laser printer. All we have to do is put our newsletter on a disk and take it to them. They only charge a few dollars to print it out on their printer. Then we take the laser-printed original and run it off on the church copier."

"Hmm." Harold thought for a moment. "If the copy shop has

✝️ first Church

P.O. Box 280 South Fork, KY 40100
"Serving God Through Serving Others"

November

Changes Made In Stewardship Campaign

The Finance Committee has revised our annual Stewardship campaign to make it easier.

Instead of the "Circuit Rider Plan" announced earlier, Stewardship Packets will again be distributed to each family. Each packet contains a "time and talent" survey and an anonymous card for financial gifts. We want everyone to understand that your financial gifts are an *estimate* of what you might give next year.

Please return your card and time and talent survey on Sunday, November 1. During the worship hour we will dedicate our gifts for the year ahead, a highlight of our annual program. The Finance Committee will be able to project a program budget based on our estimates of giving. The Administrative Council will have a pool of resource persons to draw from, based on our time and talent sheets.

Your careful planning helps the church do careful planning.

Please keep our church's stewardship program in your prayers this week. God will bless us with an abundance of resources, but we must do all in our power to make it happen.

Inside

Confirmation Class

Camp Conference Report

Good Samaritan Offering

Figure 7-1.

---

a computer like ours, we could use theirs if ours breaks down. But what if we didn't have access to a laser printer?"

"Then we'd run off our newsletters on our dot matrix printer," Bill answered. "In fact, we used our dot matrix a couple of issues ago when the copy-shop computer was down. The difference is not that objectionable."

"Our newsletter has two styles of type." Harold looked at the copy. "One style is used for headlines and the other for the text. Is that hard for the computer to do?"

"No, it's done with the push of a button," Bill said. "In fact, the computer has over twenty styles, or fonts, of type to choose from."

"Why didn't you use more than two?" Harold asked.

Bill laughed. "For the same reason you wouldn't use three or four different-colored pens in writing a letter. It would look strange."

"If you had a special issue, you could change the type style for emphasis," Harold observed.

"Sure, and we could give the layout a different appearance by going from two columns to three," Bill said. "The computer allows us to make those adjustments without destroying our basic format."

"And it's all done with just a few buttons!"

"That's right." Bill smiled. "We no longer spend hours and hours on layouts. The computer lets us see the whole page in block form. That way, we can look at the balance and white space of the layout."

"And we do our bulletins the same way," Harold added. "What about addresses? I heard we had some trouble getting them into the computer."

"Yes, because we wanted to set up a system where each address could be cross-referenced for other mailing lists," Bill replied. "We have many different mailings: congregation, officers, newsletter, choir, youth group, and so on. A cross-reference system means we don't have to enter an address more than once. That way, we save a lot of secretarial time and computer space."

"Why was it difficult to set up?" Harold wondered.

"Whenever you have a data-base system with that sort of capability, the initial setup is more complicated," Bill told him. "After you instruct the computer as to how the files are connected, the rest is simple. The secretary easily can enter addresses. Afterward, using our dot matrix printer, the computer will print out two hundred labels in less than three minutes."

"Can that same data-base program tell me what I owe on my pledge?" Harold asked.

"In a matter of seconds," Bill replied. "Our data-base program, in addition to filing addresses, keeps records and makes calculations."

"One thing I don't understand is why we have a telephone hookup to our computer."

"Oh, you mean the modem," Bill said.

"Yeah, well, whatever you call that gadget for the phone," Harold said disapprovingly. "It looks like a waste of money to me."

Networking

"Not with our church networking system," Bill said.

"What does this network do?' " Harold asked.

"It's a network of hundreds of church computers," Bill replied. "Networking gives us an inexpensive way of instantly talking back and forth via computer. Instead of calling up one person and asking for information, you can type out a computer message and get responses from any number of churches."

"What do they do? Call back on the phone?" Harold was puzzled.

"No, the phone gives you an interconnected line and the answers come back on the computer screen," Bill said. "Of course, other phone numbers let you select the individual or groups you want to talk to."

"So you type back and forth?"

"That's right," Bill said. "For example, our young people were looking for transportation to our national youth conference. We found three other churches through our network who had extra space. Also, we managed to sell our old addressing machine through this system."

"Does the minister use it?" Harold asked.

"He sure does," Bill responded. "Some seminaries are on the system, and they share information on preaching and theology."

"I suppose Harriet uses the church network for the newsletter," Harold said.

"Where do you think Harriet gets such great anecdotes and cartoons?" Bill responded.

"You mean pictures can be sent over this system and printed out on our dot matrix?" Harold was intrigued.

"Sure, if the sender has a scanner to copy the picture and a communication program to send it," Bill answered. "However, the big advantage to networking is immediate retrieval. Your mail becomes electronic. In one minute, you type out a message and send it, and in the next minute, you receive a reply. Of course, you can print out whatever you send or receive. Also, you can post a message onto an electronic 'bulletin board' open to all receivers. That's how we sold the Addressograph."

"An electronic bulletin board could also carry a request for information," Harold said. "You could find out how other churches are doing things and not have to keep reinventing the wheel. This network must cost a fortune."

"Not really," Bill replied. "There's a nominal charge for the network, but the cost of the phone is about the same as regular calls."

"So this new computer not only makes a difference in our print production but in how we communicate," Harold observed.

CONCLUSION

A good newsletter cannot be credited to the craft of a computer. A real live person must write the articles and decide on its layout. Judge your publication critically. Does it achieve its goal? How well does it capture the spirit of your church? Does it communicate information efficiently so it can be read without effort? Would you stop to read it if it came in *your* mail?

The church is a family, and the newsletter is like a letter from home. When members read it, the stories should make them feel glad to be a part of that family. An uninviting, uninteresting newsletter leaves the member with the expectation that the church provides a dull homecoming. The articles of a newsletter should bring to life the activity of the church and make outsiders want to learn more about it. Its pages should provide not only facts but the warmth, sympathy, challenge, and laughter of Christian experience.

Despite their down times, computers undoubtedly are a blessing to the church. Processing and disseminating information are a large part of what churches do. The computer makes possible the handling of information through composition of bulletins and newsletters, compilation of records, and networking in a more efficient and flexible way. The savings in time alone in doing these tasks make the computer worth the cost.

One of the most exciting and creative functions of a church media committee is advertising. However, as Harriet's committee soon will learn, a good short ad can take a lot of thought to develop.

8

Church
Advertising

The First Church Media Committee had become one of the most talked-about committees in the church. Harriet often received phone calls from members of the congregation suggesting what they might do next. One day, Rev. Bob Mackintosh called an emergency meeting of the media committee.

"I suppose you're wondering why I've called you all here," Bob began. "Our church has an exciting opportunity to do something very significant for the community. As you know, I have been doing a counseling series on TV. I have a very special guest coming in from out of town who's nationally known for her marriage clinics: Dr. Sarah Rute."

"Doctor who?" asked Harold.

"Dr. Rute!" Bob said. "She's nationally known to many, many people. I'm sure some of you have seen her on TV. Her clinics are designed so that couples learn how to share with each other and become better friends. My wife and I went to one, and it really helped us."

The members of the committee looked at each other blankly. Obviously they were unaware of Dr. Rute's reputation.

"What's important now," Bob continued, "and very exciting, is that Dr. Rute has agreed to stay over and do a weekend clinic in our church. We only have two months to prepare, and I want the media committee to get the word out to the community. I know that it's a big job, but I have confidence in you. You've done wonderful work before. I'm counting on you to bring in dozens of couples for Dr. Rute's clinic."

"Uh"—Harold tried to conceal his lack of enthusiasm—"we don't have the money to advertise."

"That's not a problem," Bob said. "Mrs. Goodworthy is making a donation to cover the cost."

Everyone in the committee liked Bob and didn't want to disappoint him, so they agreed to do the project. They knew, of course, that a media blitz of the entire community was needed. As it turned out, Mrs. Goodworthy's donation was generous but not enough to pay for every form of media—radio, TV, and newspaper advertising. They would be working within a very limited budget.

When the committee met to discuss publicity plans, Fred Wells, who had become the youth representative on the committee, made a case for building the campaign around radio.

"Unless we pay for our advertising," Fred said, "we cannot choose our time slots or the places we want our ads to appear. Selecting our spots is crucial for attracting the audience we want. We don't have enough money for a thorough multimedia coverage of our event. But we can saturate our target audience by paying for radio spots on Friday nights and Saturdays."

"What do you mean by saturate?" Mark asked.

Audience saturation

"It's like fishing," Fred answered. "You find the greatest concentration of fish and throw as many lines in the water as possible. If we bunch our spots together in a time frame when most people are listening—saturate the audience—we can maximize the use of our ads."

"What are the best times on radio?" Jane asked.

"I'm suggesting that we run three thirty-second spots on Friday evenings during drive time and six spots on Saturdays," Fred replied. "Most people listen to the radio while they are in their cars—especially going to and from work or shopping on Saturdays. Usually, they listen for no more than an hour, so you get a variety of audiences over several hours. We can develop six or seven different spots and repeat them for six consecutive weekends."

"How will you catch people's attention?" Harold asked.

"On radio, we have to break through the everyday routines of listeners and the onslaught of other electronic messages." Fred paused for a moment. "I would suggest using some catchy material with some snappy music and repeating our phone number several times to get people to call in about the clinic. We can test the effectiveness of our spots by the number of phone calls we get."

"Someone will have to stand by the phone," Martha observed.

"Right," Fred said. "If we can't handle that, we need an answering machine to give the basic info and receive messages."

"Why couldn't we do this campaign on access TV?" Mark asked.

"Hmm." Harold considered the idea. "We could announce the clinic at the end of our regular programs. However, I don't think a saturation campaign would work. Cable access provides a free community channel, so the rules focus on fair usage among participants. Several time slots selected by one group in a single day wouldn't be considered fair."

"Wait a minute." Jane spoke up. "If we prepare a one-minute TV spot for the end of our own access programs, we might get our commercial TV station to rebroadcast the spot as a public service. I know commercial TV is no longer required to do PSA's, but they still do some community spots voluntarily."

"That might work!" Harold agreed. "It wouldn't saturate the audience but it would give us double coverage for one production cost."

"The more variety of advertising we get, the better," Harriet said. "In addition, I'll prepare the usual press release for the newspaper and see if we can get some free *print* publicity."

"What's the format to use for a news release?" Bill asked, knowing Harriet's background as a newspaper editor.

"Use regular eight-and-a-half-by-eleven-inch white paper and type only on one side, double- or triple-spaced," Harriet replied. "Identify yourself and the church at the top of the page with address and phone number. When another page follows, write 'more' at the bottom of the page. At the end of the article, type '30'—a newspaper code for 'this is the end.' Also, observe these don'ts: don't send out carbon copies, don't hyphenate words, and don't split paragraphs at the end of a page."

News releases

"What are our chances of getting our news release published?" Mark asked.

"The less that is going on of importance that day, the more space will be available," Harriet said. "Of course, the newspaper editor must regard the story as newsworthy and the source as reliable. It's a good idea to call the paper first, let them get to know you, and politely find out if they will at least consider the story. I should also mention that most newspapers, in order to fit their own style, will rewrite whatever is sent in."

"It's interesting how our paid advertising relates to our free publicity," Mark commented. "We can get people's attention with our *paid* saturation campaign on radio and reinforce it with occasional *free* TV and newspaper publicity. At least that way we'll get some mileage out of the multimedia approach."

"I hope we also can run some *paid* newspaper ads," Harriet said. "There's no substitute for being able to run ads when and where we want them—and newspapers have a distinct audience that would increase the coverage of our campaign."

The committee began to implement their decisions. Jane, who had a background in drama, worked with Fred in preparing the radio scripts. They decided to write out parts for a man and a woman talking about the clinic. Because the first few seconds would make or break the spots, the opening lines were designed as attention-getters.

Radio spots

"Try this line as a grabber." Jane smiled. "The man says, 'Our marriage is not *sick;* why do I have to go to Dr. Rute's clinic?' "

"Good!" Fred responded. "Then the woman could say, 'If you loved me, you'd go. Our marriage may not be sick, but I believe in preventive medicine.' "

"Then the narrator could say, 'Treat your marriage as if *you* cared. Call 891-3400 for information on Dr. Rute's free clinic June eighth through tenth at First Church.' " Jane scribbled the lines down on paper.

"Let's repeat the number and have the narrator conclude with 'That's *891-3400*,' " Fred said. "I'll find a few seconds of jazzy music to begin and end it."

"Should we use the same music each time?" Jane asked.

"Yes. If the scripts have a little humor, the music will cue listeners for our other spots," Fred replied. "For our next spot, how about doing one on communication? The man could say to his wife, 'How come when I say something, you never answer me directly—' "

"Hold it," Jane said. "I don't like that. It puts women into a stereotype. Some women are guilty of indirect and ambiguous language, but not all of them."

"All right," Fred replied. "Then have the *woman* say the first line and let the man be guilty of equivocation."

After Fred and Jane had edited the second script on "communication," it was typed out as follows:

WOMAN:	How come when I ask you something, you always answer me with a question?
MAN:	What do you mean?
WOMAN:	You're doing it again!
MAN:	What?
WOMAN:	Answering a question with a question. How are we going to learn to communicate?
MAN:	Maybe we should go to Dr. Rute's clinic at First Church.
WOMAN:	Now there's a good answer!
NARRATOR:	Dr. Rute's clinic June eighth through tenth can be your answer too. Call 891-3400 for more information. That's 891-3400.

The fertile minds of Fred and Jane produced a total of seven scripts. For variety, the voices of several actors were used and the spots were produced on the professional equipment at the radio station.

Before releasing the spots for broadcast, Harriet tested them on several members at First Church. Mrs. Goodworthy objected to one of the spots, so it was replaced with another. Jane quipped that the media committee was following the golden rule in accommodating Mrs. Goodworthy: "She who has the gold, rules." However, no one doubted the wisdom of pretesting the spots with members of the congregation.

TV spots

Bill Henson had an idea for adapting the radio spots for TV. He admired the cartoon work of Jane Hardgrove in the church newsletters. After church one Sunday, he talked it over with her.

"I like the expressions you give to the faces of your cartoon characters," Bill said. "You can almost hear them talking. Why not do a series of color cartoons for TV and use the voices from the radio spots?"

"You mean like a talking comic strip?" Jane asked.

"Exactly," Bill replied. "You could draw the actors talking together from different angles—four or five cartoons to each script."

"Hmm." Jane visualized the concept. "The facial expressions would have to match the script. I guess I could do that, but it's a lot of work."

"Well, you wouldn't have to do all seven scripts," Bill said. "Just two or three. Our TV coverage will repeat the spots less often than radio."

"OK. If the media committee will approve the idea, I'll do it," Jane said.

The media committee, of course, unanimously approved—especially with Jane doing most of the work. After Jane finished the cartoons, Fred videotaped them and edited in the audio at Parkway Church. He also added some special effects. (Later, Sally Hawsley at the cable access studio saw the finished product and encouraged them to enter a national video contest. The promos won high honors and Jane and Fred were interviewed about their work on a local TV station.)

Meanwhile, the media committee discovered that they had just enough money after the radio spots to run a small newspaper ad for one week. Harriet, Bill, and Martha got the job of constructing it and met together to begin their work.

Newspaper ads

"I know the editor of our newspaper," Harriet said, "and maybe I can get our ad in a good section on an open page."

"What's an 'open page' and a 'good section'?" Bill asked.

"Our newspaper has three or four sections: sports, entertainment, features, and so on. Each section has a front page and a back page. Those are the pages immediately *open* to the reader's view."

"Why is one section better than another?" Bill wondered.

"It depends on the audience we're trying to reach as to which one would be best for us," Harriet answered. "For the largest number of readers, the sports or entertainment sections might be the best. However, since we are trying to reach the people most likely to come to a marriage clinic, our best choice might be the feature section."

"Often the paper doesn't give you a choice," Martha broke in.

"That's true," Harriet admitted. "All we can do is ask."

"I've never written up a newspaper ad," Bill said. "How do we begin?"

"The trick is to get the message across attractively in as few words as possible," Harriet replied.

"The use of white space will help make the ad attractive," Martha said.

"How about drawing a box around it?" Bill asked.

"That's a good idea for setting the ad apart," Harriet replied, "especially for a small ad such as ours. Let's sit back and think about the main attraction of this event. What's the one thing about it that would draw people in?"

"Would it be Dr. Rute?" Martha asked.

"From what I've seen and heard, Dr. Rute has a small but very loyal following in our community," Harriet responded. "Probably they already know about this event and are planning to come. We should mention her name in the ad but not as the lead statement."

"Then what's the appeal of the clinic?" Bill asked.

"The appeal would be to people with troubled marriages or to those with good marriages who want them to be better," Martha replied.

"Those are two different groups," Harriet said. "I'm not sure we can construct a small ad that effectively appeals to both types."

"Maybe we should approach it from a psychological angle," Martha said. "Will most people want to admit that they are part of a troubled marriage? If we advertise a clinic for 'troubled marriages,' the ad might turn off the people we are trying to reach."

"That's a good point," Harriet acknowledged.

"I like the line from one of our radio spots," Bill said. " 'Treat your marriage as if you cared.' "

"That's a winner," Martha agreed. "It doesn't offend anybody and appeals to something fundamental."

"In fact, that's about all we need to say in a small ad." Harriet smiled. "That's our message—and it reinforces what we've said on the radio."

The ad was typed out for the newspaper. (See Figure 8-1.)

Dr. Rute's clinic indeed was successful, and a large number of couples attended. During the program, members of the media committee took a survey with the question "Where did you first learn about this event?" To their surprise, the majority of participants had first heard about the clinic through word-of-mouth. The committee remembered what Sharon Norris had said about the diffusion process of media: a campaign is only successful when people start talking about it. Media create awareness, but the decision to buy into an event comes through interpersonal channels.

The second largest response to the question "Where did you first learn about this event?" was radio. The committee knew from this response and from the phone calls that the saturation campaign had worked. TV and newspaper ads also significantly showed up in the survey. Of course, the combination of radio, TV, and newspaper—reinforcing one another—increased the impact geometrically. The final result of the campaign, accounting for its success, was that the message spread to word-of-mouth.

The media committee was now convinced of the importance of advertising. After the clinic was over, Harriet called a meeting to explore how the regular programs of First Church might best be advertised.

"How can we apply what we learned from the Dr. Rute campaign to our regular church advertising?" Harriet began.

"I don't see any comparison," Harold replied. "The Rute campaign was built around a *special* event with an out-of-town expert. How would that apply to advertising the routine services we offer at First Church?"

"I learned about the importance of awareness," Martha said, "and the power of the media in creating it."

"I wonder if people in the community are aware of our church and what it has to offer?" Mark asked.

"How would you test that?" Jane wanted to know.

Figure 8-1. Newspaper ad.

"We might find out by asking people in the community," Fred responded.

"Asking them what?" Harold wondered.

"Wait a minute," Bill said. "I'm getting an idea. When I was new to the community, I asked a clerk in a grocery store where I could find First Church. The store was only four blocks away, but the clerk had never heard of the church. It was as if it didn't exist."

"Hmm." Harriet smiled. "I remember a question from philosophy. 'If a tree falls in the forest and no one hears it, does the sound of it exist?' Or for that matter, if a church exists in a community and no one knows about it, does

Awareness of location

it exist?"

"Well, it won't exist for very long if no one knows about it," Martha concluded. "We have to advertise."

"I question the validity of Bill's one-person survey," Harold said. "You're forgetting about the media campaign we just completed. I'll bet that grocery clerk knows about us now."

"I haven't finished yet," Bill said. "We could easily survey the businesses in our neighborhood. One question would do it: 'Can you tell me where First Church is?' "

"Even with the success of the Rute campaign, the answer to that question could still be no," Harriet said. "People may have become aware of Dr. Rute's clinic but not of the location of the church."

"Our purpose in that campaign was not to make people aware of our location," Martha added, "but to have them call for more information about the clinic."

"Why didn't we give our location?" Mark asked.

"In a short ad, you have to stick to one purpose," Harriet replied. "If you crowd in too much information, you overload the audience."

"A good ad works like a rifle, not a shotgun," Fred agreed.

"Well, maybe now we need a rifle that targets our location," Mark said.

"Before we do anything, I want to see if Bill is right," Harold said. "I'm not convinced that the business people in our neighborhood are unaware of our existence."

"All right," Harriet replied. "Let's each take a few stores and ask the owner, 'Can you tell me where First Church is?' "

The members of the media committee agreed to this proposition and completed the survey in two weeks' time. There were only twenty-one stores to cover. To Harold's chagrin, none of the people in the stores he visited knew where his church was. At one point, he exclaimed in exasperation, "Look, you can see the steeple of the church from your window!" To which the owner replied, "If you knew where it was, why did you ask me in the first place?"

Other members of the committee had much the same results as Harold. Out of twenty-one neighborhood businesses, only three knew the location of First Church. When the committee met again, they were humbler but wiser.

"I can't believe that our church has been nonexistent in this neighborhood for thirty years!" Martha said.

"People notice what's important to them," Jane reasoned. "If they aren't members of our denomination, why should we expect them to know where we are?"

"What bothers me," Harold said, "is that newcomers, asking for information about us, are not going to get it even from the neighborhood gas station."

"How can we correct that?" Harriet asked.

"One thing we might do," Bill replied, "is put up a road sign."

"Yes, but the city restricts the location of signs," Harold said.

"Even if we did get permission from the city," Mark added, "we would be competing in a jungle of other signs."

"If we can find a place for it, putting up a sign is a good idea," Harriet said, "but it's not enough. We would still have our problem. For many of our neighbors, our church doesn't exist. What sort of advertising can we do to change that?"

"Let me repeat my point," Jane insisted. "If our church is unimportant to nonmembers, why should they want to know our location? How can you target an advertising campaign to an indifferent audience?"

Awareness of importance

"Maybe our friendship is important to at least some people in the community," Bill countered. "Loneliness can be a big problem."

"That suggests a possible approach," Fred said. "We could build a campaign around the slogan 'You have a friend at First Church.'"

"I'm proud of the way our church has developed a spirit of friendliness and community," Martha said. "Our new greeters on Sunday morning have certainly made a difference. And newcomers can see what we are doing to help others from our picture displays in the hallway and from the church newsletter."

"But what can we say in an *ad* that really makes friendship important?" Jane persisted.

"That's a good question," Harriet replied. "Our last campaign started off with you and Fred working on radio scripts. Maybe you two can come up with something on the importance of friendship."

"I really doubt that we can make this friendship angle work," Jane objected.

"Yes, we can!" Fred insisted. "I've already got some ideas. What have we got to lose by trying?"

"OK, I guess we can try," Jane conceded.

In the following week, Fred and Jane debated with each other about proposed scripts. Finally, Fred came up with one that Jane liked. It was developed around the theme of finding a friend:

MAN: People don't care. I don't have any *real* friends.
WOMAN: I do.
MAN: How do you know they care?
WOMAN: They listen to my problems, come to see me when I'm sick, and take my kids to camp.
MAN: Wow! Where do you get friends like that?
WOMAN: At First Church.
NARRATOR: You too have a friend at First Church—Main and Willow Streets, four blocks east of Merchants Mall.

After they had looked at this script for a while, Jane pointed out why she thought it was a good one.

"This script describes the importance of friendship without preaching about it," Jane said. "That's good. But better than that, it creates an image of caring that makes the listener want to become a part of it. I developed another script with a different approach. Take a look and see what you think."

WOMAN: Fill in the blank. Friendship is—
MAN: —throwing a Frisbee with my dog, Rex.
WOMAN: I never see you with people.
MAN: Show me someone I can trust more than my dog.
WOMAN: All right, I'll take you with me to First Church next Sunday.
MAN: Can they catch a Frisbee?
WOMAN: I don't know, but I think you'll like how they catch the Spirit.
NARRATOR: You have a friend at First Church—Main and Willow Streets, four blocks east of Merchants Mall.

Fred looked at the script. "I like that. Your use of humor keeps the church from looking old-fashioned, while suggesting that there is more to life than throwing a Frisbee."

"Of course, the most important thing is that we are attaching a positive image to the location of the church. The whole point of these ads is to catch people's attention and make them aware of where we are."

"Right," Fred said. "People have to feel that there is something important about our church before they take note of our location."

The media committee looked over the scripts that Fred and Jane prepared. They had some reservations.

"How come you don't give our time of services and phone number?" Mark asked.

"We can do that in our newspaper ads," Jane replied. "But remember what we said during our last campaign about overloading a thirty-second radio spot with too much information."

"It's especially hard for a radio listener to remember much," Martha said.

"That's correct," Jane answered. "In fact, we'll be lucky if the members of the radio audience retain a vague image of First Church as being somewhere around Merchants Mall. It's easier to absorb information about our time of services from the newspaper."

"We also can reinforce what you are doing on radio with our newspaper ads," Harriet said. "I've written down something I think will work."

The committee members looked at Harriet's proposal for a newspaper ad:

YOU HAVE A FRIEND
AT FIRST CHURCH
Corner of Willow
and Main
Four blocks east
of Merchants Mall
Church school: 10 A.M.
Worship service: 11A.M.
891-3400

"That's the information we want people to have," Mark said emphatically. "If it's too much for radio, how about putting it at the end of our TV access programs?"

"We already have our address and phone number included in the final credits," Harold said. "The credits roll by too fast to add the other information. Maybe we can get Bob Mackintosh to conclude his programs with 'Remember, you have a friend at First Church. Come visit us at our eleven o'clock worship service.' "

"I'll go along with that," Mark agreed.

"What really would be great is to get the evangelism committee working with us," Martha suggested. "Maybe they could organize a campaign to encourage members to bring a friend to First Church."

"Sure." Bill seconded the motion. "The evangelism committee could declare a Friendship Month. We could put up posters in the hallways saying YOU HAVE A FRIEND AT FIRST CHURCH. Then our newsletter could come out with articles about bringing a friend to church."

"That's a good idea," Harriet said. "Perhaps our minister would start the month with a special sermon on friendship. During the month, he could remind the congregation of our campaign with announcements from the pulpit."

The media committee completed its plans for the campaign and enthusiastically presented it to the board. However, the board did not feel that the budget would allow for a media campaign until the following year. At first the media committee was disheartened, but finally they regained their momentum and developed another campaign for internally marketing the idea to the congregation. They produced the radio spots on church equipment and played them within a special presentation to the evangelism committee. After that, Harriet repeated the same presentation at a fellowship supper.

When the board saw the idea catching fire with other members of the congregation, they approved the campaign for the current year. (Often an innovative approach must be internally marketed in just this way before a committee is allowed to implement it.) Furthermore, with the congregation solidly behind the campaign, the results were much more assured. How the board assessed the overall work of the media committee is a story for the next chapter.

CONCLUSION

Advertising is equally important on all levels of the institutional church. The general public apparently has little awareness of the importance of the local church. Probably, the public sees most churches as self-serving entities struggling to keep "organized religion" alive. Rarely does the image of the church come across as sacrificially giving itself for the betterment of people. More likely, the church is regarded as the bastion of morality, encrusted in its own tradition and oblivious to the needs of outsiders. However, if the local church can project itself through media as truly serving "the least of these," then people will become aware and start to listen.

Advertising is a means to an end, not an end unto itself—just as using media is a means to an end. It would be foolish to purchase land for farming and then to eschew the tools for farming. It is not enough to believe in the mission of the church; we must use the tools at hand to communicate that mission. Advertising provides tools: radio, TV, and newspapers. Just as a failure to learn the use of farm tools means a poor harvest, so it is with the tools of advertising—we cannot sow or reap in today's mission without their skillful use.

The problem of some denominations with advertising is in the need for simplicity. Advertising does not provide an effective means for reaffirming doctrinal beliefs. Its messages must be short and easily grasped by the public. There is no platform for the great theologian within radio, TV, and newspaper ads. Advertising merely opens the door for such dialogue; it will not deliver the message. As a result, even the best church ads will appear trivial in content. However, the issue is not so much one of content as of appeal.

An appealing ad, repeated many times, opens the door in a way that doctrinal content cannot. It comes across like Jesus' greeting to the little man sitting in a tree for a better view: "Zacchaeus, come down! I'm going to eat at your house today." The best church ads will have that same personal touch. What is needed is a warm, friendly invitation meant just for the person out on a limb, estranged from the church. The most difficult job may be in convincing respectable church members that such an invitation should be delivered.

The media committee at First Church has learned how to send out information through the media. However, the church also must learn how to link its usage of media with the interpersonal life of the congregation. The committee examines this vital function in the next chapter.

9

Linking Media to the Interpersonal Church

One of the big problems of churches is that members tend to compartmentalize their work. People become so focused on one specific area of the church—the music program, for example, or the church school, or stewardship, or social outreach—that they may grow blind to the rest. Although the media committee thought they had done an excellent job in their first two years, not all board members considered the media program important. In fact, one or two protested that the media committee had used funds that better could have been spent elsewhere.

The media committee was very disappointed when Rev. Bob Mackintosh informed them that they must prepare a careful defense of their work in order to receive funding for the next year. They felt the worth of their efforts should have been obvious to all.

"If there's one thing I can't stand, it's ingratitude," Harold said as the media committee began its meeting.

"I know how you feel," Harriet told him, "but look at it this way. We know our work is important, and now we have the opportunity to prove it."

"How are we going to do that?" Martha asked. "We already have the most visible program in church. What more can we do to show them the worth of media?"

"Well, we can point to increased attendance at church, better participation in committees and programs, and more new members," Fred asserted.

"Some of our board members are claiming that those increases are due to word-of-mouth," Martha said.

"Of course they're due to word-of-mouth!" Jane exclaimed.

"But it was our use of the media that created the awareness to start people talking in the first place!"

"We all talk about the high visibility of media," Martha said. "The irony of it is that using the media becomes invisible in the final result—interpersonal decisions. So how can we prove its value?"

"Somehow our use of media has got to link up with the interpersonal life of the congregation," Mark said.

Jane was puzzled. "I'm not sure what you're saying."

"I'm not either." Mark laughed. "I just said it."

"Mark may be intuitively pointing us in the right direction," Harriet said reflectively. "We have to find some way of disclosing the interpersonal worth of media use within our congregation."

"Here's another way of putting it," Mark said. "We need to show how using the media gives us the tools to perform the mission of the church."

"Maybe we could do some sort of video documentary of our work," Fred suggested.

"How about a video yearbook?" Jane asked.

"Now we're getting somewhere," Harold said enthusiastically. "We have video clips from the tapes we've stored featuring the various programs of our church. We might begin with those."

"Some of those tapes were erased," Fred said. "I wish we had thought of this idea earlier. We could have recorded some of the better clips from each show on a single storage tape— what TV stations call 'file footage.'"

"Well, at least we can do that for next year," Harold said.

"Let me see if I understand." Harriet paused. "We're proposing a yearbook type of presentation that we would videotape for the board. We would demonstrate how we successfully have interpreted the overall mission of our local church."

Producing a video yearbook

"The importance of this project," Mark broke in, "is that this yearbook would allow all members of the congregation to see what others are doing. Most of us are so wrapped up in our own areas of interest that we can't see the forest for the trees."

"Think what this yearbook would mean to new members," Jane said. "They would get a graphic idea of the full impact of our church. No matter what program they decide to join, they would still have a visual introduction to our total organization."

"This tape also would be perfect for Homecoming Day," Bill said. "It would give everyone the big picture."

"All right, then we're agreed." Harriet smiled. "Let's get started. What sorts of things do we want to include in our yearbook?"

"We'll want to represent all our program areas," Martha said.

"But we don't have to be boring about it," Bill added. "Instead of talking about what we do, let's show it. The narrator can lead into clips of people actually doing the work."

"I wonder if we can do some interviews of people that the church has benefited in its work with illiteracy, the homeless, the day-care program, and other such areas?" Mark asked.

"What might be better than interviews are testimonials," Jane suggested. "The program would have more impact if these people were facing the camera and talking directly to the audience. We wouldn't have to limit the talks to social concerns; we could include members telling about their enjoyment of such programs as the choir, senior citizens, and camping."

"That's good, but we don't want one talking head right after another," Harold said. "For variety, I think we should use both testimonials and interviews. Most important, each statement should lead into a clip of the actual program. We should see the choir singing and the kids around a campfire."

"Of course, we can use other visuals such as photos and graphics to fill in for programs without video clips," Fred added.

"To give the yearbook an inspirational calendar look, we can use material from our celebrations during Christmas, Easter, Pentecost, and Thanksgiving," Bill said.

"Let's not forget to include the work of our wonderful board." Martha laughed.

"We need a framework to develop these ideas," Harriet said. "I suggest that we get a script put together by—"

"Fred and Jane!" the others said in chorus.

"Right. And then maybe Harold will act as our executive producer for the video clips and the talent."

"I would want to go through the video material that we have on hand before writing the script," Fred said.

"I'll help you look through it," Harold volunteered.

After the video footage was researched from past programs, Fred and Jane went to work on the script.

"I keep coming back to the same idea for an opening and closing," Jane said. "I visualize Bob Mackintosh sitting by his fireplace with a book that says YEARBOOK on the cover."

Fred laughed. "Is there a dog holding slippers in his mouth?"

"Well, a yearbook is something you enjoy reading," Jane replied. "If you don't like the fireplace, maybe we could have him sitting in his office."

"I agree the minister should open and close the show," Fred said. "And the yearbook is a good idea if we don't get too corny."

"All right," Jane conceded. "How about having Bob seated in a comfortable chair away from his desk. His opening line could be, 'I have just received a wonderful gift from our media committee.' Then he could point to the yearbook."

"I like that," Fred said. "His next line might be, 'What you are about to see gives the big picture of a small but important congregation.'"

"That's good," Jane said. "Then he could make a simple transition into the first segment: 'This yearbook follows the Christian year and begins with Advent at First Church.'"

"Following the Christian year is all right," Fred said. "But we don't want people to think that the only time our church is alive is during Christmas and Easter."

"That's true," Jane said, "but I was thinking of the full Christian year: Advent, Christmas, Lent, Easter, and Pentecost."

Fred grinned. "I've got some great footage from a New Year's party with our youth group."

"Our church has a lot of fun together and we don't want to leave those times out," Jane agreed. "But our main purpose is to show what we are doing in our mission. This is not a thirty-second ad to catch people's attention."

"No argument there," Fred said.

As it turned out, not all the significant events at First Church could be linked to the Christian year. However, there were enough visuals to show the movement from one season to another. The production plan was developed for a thirty-minute program, with the possibility of a shorter second version to be edited from the first. The outline was as follows:

Segment 1: Opening, 1 minute
   A. Opening titles and music (30 seconds)
   B. Comment by minister, seated in office with yearbook (30 seconds)

Segment 2: Advent, 5 minutes

A. Video clip of a child lighting first Advent candle with short explanation of meaning from narrator (1 minute)

B. Transition by narrator to statement by chairperson of Board; show photos of the board and programs supported (2 minutes)

C. Transition by narrator to chairperson of Community Outreach, with video clip of members helping the homeless (1 minute)

D. Cut to chairperson of Stewardship, who talks about other examples of where money goes to help people (1 minute)

Segment 3: Christmastide, 5 minutes

A. Video clip of choir singing during candlelight service (1 minute)

B. Transition by narrator to video clip of church carolers going from house to house (1 minute)

C. Cut to Mission chairperson, who talks about special Christmas offering; edit in photos of persons helped (1 minute)

D. Transition by narrator to youth group party at New Year's (30 seconds)

E. Transition by narrator to minister's work in the prison ministry; mention audiocassette ministry (1½ minutes)

Segment 4: Lent (5 minutes)

A. Interview with choir director explaining Lenten theme and music (1 minute)

B. Video clip of choir singing cantata (1 minute)

C. Transition by narrator to chairperson of Ecumenical Committee; show photos of churches working together in housing project (1½ minutes)

D. Transition by narrator to video clip of homebound person expressing appreciation for audiocassette ministry; also show video clip of young people working with audio equipment (1½ minutes)

Segment 5: Eastertide (5 minutes)

A. Video clip of Easter choir processional (30 seconds)

B. Cut to minister, who talks about Easter services (1 minute)

C. Transition by narrator to interview with Harriet Wingate and chairperson of Evangelism to tell how the Media and Evangelism committees worked together; show photos of new members' class (2 minutes)

D. Transition by narrator to 30-second TV ad for Dr. Rute's marriage clinic, with short statement by Mrs. Goodworthy of why she helped fund the clinic through the Media Committee; show photos of clinic attendance (1½ minutes)

Segment 6: Pentecost (6½ minutes)

A. Video clip shows Pentecost celebration; narrator explains the birthday of the church and the meaning of Pentecost (1 minute)

B. Transition by narrator to video clip of church retreat at a campsite (30 seconds)

C. Cut to youth director, who talks about youth camping; show video footage and photos (1 minute)

D. Transition by narrator to video clip of teacher training class (30 seconds)

E. Cut to church school superintendent, who talks about Sunday school classes; show photos of classes and visuals of curriculum materials (2½ minutes)

F. Cut to chairperson of Board, who talks about the training of church officers; show photos of class (1 minute)

Segment 7: Closing (2½ minutes)

A. Begin with one-line testimonials; use variety of ages and types of people on what the church has meant to them (1 minute)

B. Wrap up with minister (1 minute)

C. End titles and music (½ minute)

Developing a script from the production plan was a relatively simple task. Putting together the visuals and talent took somewhat longer. Finally, the yearbook was completed and ready for presentation to the board. However, the board resisted the idea of taking up their meeting time with a thirty-minute videotape. Therefore, Harriet presented the full version of the yearbook at the congregation's monthly fellowship supper and an edited version of ten minutes was presented to the board.

When the board met, several of its members already had seen the full version at the fellowship supper. They informed the other members of what they were missing by not watching the whole program.

"It is too bad that our board chose not to see the yearbook in its entirety," one board member told the committee. "You certainly proved to me how valuable the media committee is to our church. What you are doing is essential to the work of all our programs."

"Well, we saw the truth of that in the ten-minute version," replied another board member. "It answers the question of why our church work is so important. I'd like a copy to show some of my friends who wonder why I spend so much time at church."

"I'm going to show the full version on the access channel," Bob Mackintosh said. "I think the yearbook says more about our church in thirty minutes than any of us could say in a year."

"From week to week, we don't realize how much our church

does," another board member said. "The yearbook makes us aware of the total picture. I hope the media committee will make this an annual project."

"What I didn't realize," the chairperson said, "is how intimately the media committee is linked to our other programs. It tells the story of each of our mission areas. Really, the media committee is not a separate program of the church but provides a service to us all. Each program area should have a budget item for media."

"The great thing about this videotape," another board member said, "is that it is not limited to one presentation. I like the idea of two versions; we can use both. I suspect that some of our members will be wanting copies."

Harriet smiled. "We already have had a number of requests."

"Well, you've made your point," the chairperson said. "The yearbook tells the story not only of the church but of the splendid work of our media committee. Cutting off your funds would cut off our right to communicate what the church does. We'll make sure that doesn't happen."

CONCLUSION

Two of the biggest mistakes a church can make are not letting the community see and hear what the church is doing and not letting members within the church know what all the others are doing. Church members are often not aware of the full impact of the church. Media use within the church has the power of looking back, putting together the bits and pieces, and letting us see the entire puzzle as an important picture.

There is no doubt that using media develops a spirit of community and cohesion within the church. Media programs also have the power of conferring status to those previously ignored. The apostle Paul warns us "not to become weary of well-doing." Lack of appreciation plays a large part in such weariness. Media presentations can show church members at work and make them want to continue their good efforts.

Often members will not know what the minister is doing. Jokes about ministers working only on Sundays highlight the problem. A good media program that covers the scope of the church's mission stops the laughing. The issue is not ego satisfaction but interpretation and appreciation of mission. Stewardship ceases to exist when members cannot see and hear what is being done.

The more senses media programs bring into play, the greater the awareness and gratitude for the church. The more forms of media used—radio, TV, newspapers, cassettes, newsletters, computer networking—the greater our understanding. With repeated messages through the media reinforcing our awareness, the church becomes visible and important.

Media use can never replace the interpersonal church. Certainly we do not want an electronic ministry that seeks to substitute its medium for the community of believers. What is needed is an awareness of that community and an extension of its ministry. Active, systematic, and skilled use of the media will perform those tasks as nothing else can.

Additional Reading

Armer, Alan A. *Directing Television and Film.* Belmont, Calif.: Wadsworth Publishing Co., 1986.

Avery, R., and T. A. McCain. *Inter/Media.* 2nd ed. New York: Oxford University Press, 1986.

Baehr, Theodore. *Getting the Word Out.* San Francisco: Harper & Row, 1986. A general text on communication for churches.

Brown, Aubrey N., Jr. *The Church Publicity Book: Techniques for Communication.* Nashville: Abingdon Press. Helpful assistance to strengthen communication through printed word, AV's, telephone, and suggested public media outlets.

Community Television Review. National Federation of Local Cable Programmers, 906 Pennsylvania Avenue, SE, Washington, DC 20003.

Compaine, Benjamin M., ed. *Understanding New Media: Trends and Issues in Electronic Distribution of Information.* Cambridge, Mass.: Ballinger Publishing Co., 1984.

Copyright and You. Same address. Excellent resource on copyright laws.

Corporate Television. International Television Association (ITVA), 6311 N. O'Connor Road, Suite 110, Irving, TX 75039. Informative articles for finding out about new formats and trends.

First Steps: A Common Sense Guide to Electronic Media. Presbyterian Church (U.S.A.).

Get the Word Heard. Office of Communication, Christian Church (Disciples of Christ), P.O. Box 1986, Indianapolis, IN 46206. A radio kit manual including eight 30-minute audiocassettes and a 23-page manual.

Guidelines for Communications, 1989–1992. Cokesbury Service Center, 201 Eighth Avenue, South, Nashville, TN 37202. For local church leaders.

Hawkins, R., and S. Pingree. *Television and Behavior: Ten Years of Scientific Progress and Implications for the Eighties,* Vol. 2: Technical Reviews. Rockville, Md.: National Institute of Mental Health, 1982.

Holland, Daniel W., J. Ashton Nickerson, and Terry Vaughn. *Using Nonbroadcast Video in the Church.* Valley Forge, Pa.: Judson Press, 1980. In-house TV productions.

Katz, E. "The Two Step Flow of Communication: An Up-to-Date Report on a Hypothesis" in Robert O. Carlson, ed., *Communications and Public Opinion,* pp. 344–361. New York: Praeger, 1975.

Metzler, Ken. *Creative Interviewing.* Englewood Cliffs, N.J.: Prentice-Hall, 1978. A classic textbook on interviewing.

Miller, Jerome K. *Church Copyright Kit.* Copyright Information Services, 440 Tucker Avenue, P.O. Box 1460, Friday Harbor, WA 98250. Contains a 60-minute audiocassette and an assortment of booklets and publications dealing with video copyright for churches, fair use guidelines, videotaping off the air, and duplicating sheet music for use in meetings and social gatherings.

———. *Video Copyright Guidelines.* Presbyterian Church (U.S.A.), 100 Witherspoon Street, Louisville, KY 40202-1396. For pastors and church workers.

Millimeter. P.O. Box 95759, Cleveland, OH 44101. Professional magazine on video and film production.

Parker, Roger C. *The Aldus Guide to Basic Design.* Seattle: Aldus Corp., 1987. Basic design book for printed publications—great for designing newsletters.

Religious Public Relations Handbook. Religious Public Relations Council, P.O. Box 315, Gladwyne, PA 19035 (1988). News releases, newsletters, advertising, use of media.

Sumrall, Velma, and Lucille Germany. *Telling the Story of the Local Church.* New York: Seabury Press, 1979. Newsletters, advertising, filmmaking.

Swann, Charles. *The Communicating Church.* Office of Media Communications, Presbyterian Church in the U.S., 1981. Newsletters, bulletins, advertising, media usage.

Video Systems. 9221 Quivira Road, Overland Park, KS 66212. Professional magazine primarily for small TV studios, with how-to articles on how to go beyond the basics.

Wurtzel, Alan. *Television Production.* 2nd ed. New York: McGraw-Hill Book Co., 1983. Excellent textbook on production for advanced users.